Fire Over Israel

Fire Over Israel

Supernatural Happenings & Miracles

Gerald Derstine

Erratum
The statistical figures on numbers of converts given in
this book are incorrect as they reflect information given
to Dr. Derstine. This was based on the misunderstanding
what a "new convert" is to an Arab's understanding. To
them a new convert is one who has ceased to go to the
mosque and started reading the Bible. To Dr. Derstine a
convert is one who is born again. Therefore some of the
statistics on newly saved are not reliable.

Treasure House

a division of

Destiny Image
P.O. Box 310
Shippensburg, PA 17257

"For where your treasure is
there will your heart be also." Matthew 6:21

ISBN 1-56043-772-3

For Worldwide Distribution
Printed in the U.S.A.

First Printing: 1993   Third Printing: 1994
Second Printing: 1994

Treasure House books are available through these fine distributors outside the United States:

Christian Growth, Inc.	Successful Christian Living
Jalan Kilang-Timor, Singapore 0315	Capetown, Rep. of South Africa
Lifestream	Vision Resources
Nottingham, England	Ponsonby, Auckland, New Zealand
Rhema Ministries Trading	WA Buchanan Company
Randburg, South Africa	Geebung, Queensland, Australia
Salvation Book Centre	Word Alive
Petaling, Jaya, Malaysia	Niverville, Manitoba, Canada

Inside the U.S., call toll free to order:
1-800-722-6774

Joanne Derstine Hellier, co-author of *Following the Fire*, autobiography of Gerald Derstine, has enhanced the readability of the encounters recorded in this book through her gifted ability to write and communicate these events to the reader.

Acknowledgments

Allow me to give special thanks to all the very committed prayer intercessors who meet daily, early in the morning, at the Christian Retreat Conference Center, Bradenton, FL. My life remains on this earth because fellow servants and friends faithfully remind God to place a hedge of protection around both Beulah and me.

Strength and courage rise within my spirit as our brothers and sisters in the Holy Land villages remind me of the hours of prayer they share to uphold God's hand of blessing upon the efforts of Christian Retreat and Gospel Crusade ministries.

Thanks to the dedicated partners who faithfully give of their money, time and prayers, enabling this minstry to impact our world for more than 40 years.

My wife Beulah and our family members have been patient, spending many days and weeks in fasting and prayer when I visit hostile Moslem communities with our Arab brothers as a witness to God's grace.

Our greatest admiration and thanks go to the heavenly Father, His Son Jesus Christ, the Holy Spirit and His Word which holds together all the parts of His will and plan that he has chosen to perform upon this earth in our time and throughout Eternity.

Contents

Foreword

Could God choose an obscure factory worker from eastern Pennsylvania to bring deliverance to a nation? Handicapped by a speech impediment and an inferiority complex, Gerald Derstine would appear an unlikely candidate.

Yet throughout the Bible, God has delighted in selecting society's insignificants to accomplish His will. Perhaps they are more pliant in His hands, more reliant on His strength rather than on their own.

We remember David, the shepherd boy who was crowned king of Israel...Joseph who, though brutalized by his brothers, was later honored as leader of a nation...Esther, the orphan who became queen...Rahab, the prostitute who helped deliver a nation...the young lad whose lunch basket fed five thousand.... The list is endless.

God's Word says that He uses the foolish things of the world to confound the wise (I Cor. 1:27).

I helped my father, Gerald Derstine, write his autobiography *Following the Fire*, which was published in 1980.

In some ways, it was like replaying a tape recording in my head. During my growing-up years, I had heard his astounding account of God's visitation to his Mennonite church in 1955—oh, hundreds of times.

As the first of Gerald and Beulah's four children (and the only daughter), I was part of the story. To this day, I hold flashes of memory from that phenomenal outpouring of the Holy Spirit during the first week of 1955. I was only three-and-half years old, but certain scenes remain vivid in my mind. I thank God for that, because for those who are skeptical, I can verify the events—bizarre as they may be.

Except for a few years when I worked as a staffwriter at a local daily newspaper, I have been a part of my father's ministry since its beginning. I have seen him establish churches and hundreds of mission outreaches around the world. Like most visionaries pioneering a new work, he focuses passionately on that project, sometimes to the temporary exclusion of all others.

Gerald Derstine's work in Israel has been no different. In fact, some people have accused him of being "obsessed" with this current mission outreach. Perhaps. But I believe his heart and motives are pure, and that once again God is using Dad's compassionate and direct style to reach people who otherwise never would have been reached with the gospel. I have accompanied my father and mother many times to the Middle East and, truly, the love that they are shown by the people of Israel cuts through political, ethnic, religious and socioeconomic barriers.

God has had His blessing on this humble family's ministry from the beginning. We are acquainted with miracles, though no less awed by the supernatural when it occurs. In *Following the Fire*, my father tells of his own miracle healing of chronic stuttering. After six weeks of publicly claiming God's promise that he was already healed, he woke one morning with the physical manifestation—he truly *was* healed!

Our Savior, who performed miracles when He walked this earth, said in John 14:12 that not only would we do His works, but also "greater works than these." I believe a childlike trust, acceptance and love that "believeth all things" helps usher in God's miracle power (see I Cor. 13).

Yes, there may be some who would deceive us and take advantage of the trust we place in them. God will be the judge on that account. Our assignment, however, is to boldly love and lead people into a saving knowledge of Him, wherever the doors may open.

So read the following story with an open mind, ready to receive what God can do for you. Not only will you be amazed at the stories of miracles, but you'll also be enlightened by Gerald Derstine's keen insight into Bible prophecy as it relates to Israel, the Christian and the end-time.

Above all, may you through these pages discover your purpose as a peacemaker here on earth through our Messiah, Jesus Christ.

—Joanne Derstine Hellier

Introduction

My autobiography, *Following the Fire*, published in 1980, documents the events of my early life. It includes the phenomenal supernatural happenings that took place during the time of my pastorate in the Mennonite Church at Ogema, Minnesota, in 1954 and 1955. The book also records the prophetic words spoken in 1955 that declared a coming spiritual awakening that would affect all the nations of the world. I distinctly recall thinking at the time that those words appeared so far out and seemingly impossible to believe. I would not repeat them and even attempted to forget them.

The Spirit of the Almighty One, however, would not allow me to forget those words. It is only because of the events that happened in my life through the decades of the 80's that I could dispel the doubt in my heart and mind; I am living to see the hand of God stretched toward the most sensitive, prophecy-ridden land area on the earth. That land heralds the origin of the history of our present, existing nations.

Today the world stands in bewilderment as it views the strange events attached to the breakup of the Soviet Union states and the Communist bloc nations of eastern Europe. Only the godly are rejoicing as they behold the new beginnings following the fortieth anniversary of the state of Israel: May 14, 1988.

In his Gospel, Matthew recorded the words of our Master that spoke of His disciples needing to discern the *signs of the times.* The same is true in our day; signs continue to manifest unveiling prophecy. Christ's Body must *stop, look* and *listen*—and see the glorious mighty hand of our God manipulate the nations, forcing them to come under the umbrella of a one-world leader, if they hope to survive.

Today's generation is the one witnessing the transition of the fulfillment of the Gentile Age. This era originated with the issues of the peoples occupying the land that God calls "*My land,*" *Israel,* nearly 2,600 years ago during the time of King Nebuchadnezzar of Babylon, which is now Iraq.

The contents of this book describe the phenomenal move of God transpiring in this present time, in the same location, where in ancient times such moves altered the course of human events. Note the prophetic words of Jesus as recorded in Luke 21:24, and know that historically, since 1967, the Jewish state of Israel is governed once again from its ancient capital city, Jerusalem. "And they shall fall by the edge of the sword, and shall be led away captive into all nations: and Jerusalem shall be trodden down of the Gentiles, until the times of the Gentiles be fulfilled."

We should have no doubt that this is the generation being conditioned to see and participate in the most glorious happenings, preparing the world for the Prince of Peace, Yeshua Hameshiah.

The state of Israel today contains and governs the inhabitants of the *land* God has appointed to originate *His* redemptive plan for the human race. Biblically, we know that the same *land* has been chosen by God to consummate or finalize His great plan of restoration and redemption.

The word was declared plainly by God's angels during the moments of His ascension on the Mount of Olives next to Jerusalem:

> *...Ye men of Galilee, why stand ye gazing up into heaven? this same Jesus, which is taken up from you into heaven, shall so come in like manner as ye have seen Him go into heaven.*

> Acts 1:11

> *And His feet shall stand in that day upon the Mount of Olives, which is before Jerusalem on the east....*

> Zechariah 14:4

Today a serious problem of peace exists in this land. However, there is a people who claim to have and know the answer—they boldly declare that *Christ is the answer!* Only holy people qualify to resolve the problem on *holy land.*

Prayerfully, carefully, read the events presented in this book and attempt to understand the scriptural interpretation. As you do so, I believe a fresh anointing, a beginning, will awaken within you.

The supernatural happenings recorded in this book that involved both my wife and myself are documented by people's personal testimonies, on video tape, from their own locations in Israel and the West Bank territories.

This book is difficult to finish because supernatural happenings still continue to take place. Surely this is only the beginning of the *end*. Much, much more is coming! Look up! Our total redemption is drawing nigh. *Maranatha*!

Chapter One

The First Arab Moslem Connection

It was noontime on a picture-perfect fall day in 1981. At the Jaffa Gate's entrance to the Old City of Jerusalem, the narrow streets teemed with tourists and pilgrims who came to celebrate the Jewish holiday of Succot, the Feast of Tabernacles.

Jewish men with their black-and-white-striped prayer shawls draped around their necks held tightly to the hands of their young sons as they hurried toward the Western Wall to pray. Brushing by them were Arabs in their robes and kaffiyehs, hawking their wares in the bazaar or scurrying toward the mosque of Aqsa, above the Jewish wailing wall.

Donkeys, carts, buses, taxis and bicycles all vied for space on the crowded street, while a tourist group with matching hats and travel bags huddled around a lecturing guide.

My wife Beulah and I savored the colorful sights and sounds of the bustling, ancient city as we lunched in a tiny cafe just inside the Old City walls.

The tour members in the group we hosted were enjoying a "free morning," and we had looked forward to a few private moments.

Taking a bite from my sandwich, I suddenly caught the glance of a stranger standing a polite distance from our table. At least four times our eyes met. Then he edged over to where my wife and I sat.

Staring at the bronze "Blessings" pin fastened to my coat lapel, he asked, "Where did you get that?"

"I make them," I said.

"You make them?"

"Yes," I replied, "I give them to the people who help me in the work I do."

Pondering for a moment, he then asked, "Where did you get that word 'Blessings'? I like that word; it does something for me."

"That word comes from the Holy Book," I replied, "the words of Jesus, who said, 'It is more blessed to give than to receive.' "

"May I buy one from you?" the stranger asked.

"No, they're not for sale," I told him.

Pausing momentarily, the man studied my face and then boldly remarked, "You are a good man."

"What do you mean, I'm a 'good man'? You don't know my name and I don't know who you are. How can you say I'm a good man?"

"I can tell by your eyes," he quickly replied. "You are an honest man."

Then, before I could reply, he asked, "May I borrow this pin from you? Come back in four hours and I will show you something you like. I will return your pin and give you a gift."

I looked at Beulah. She was smiling, and her eyes said, "Why not?" So, intrigued by the man's offer, I handed him the pin. He may be conning me, I thought, but it was no great loss. I had plenty more pins back home.

Four hours later, true to his word, the young man returned the pin, as well as an exquisite silver necklace. The word "Blessings," a duplicate etching of my lapel pin, dangled from the delicate chain.

"This is for you," he said, white teeth gleaming in a wide smile, as he handed the piece of jewelry to my wife.

"No, I will pay for it," she said, but just as quickly he replied, "I don't need the money, I'll give it to you."

As Beulah admired her special gift, the man asked how many ladies were accompanying our tour group. "Twenty-six ladies," I replied.

"Tonight I will bring to your hotel 26 silver necklaces, one for each lady," he responded. Indeed, late that night this man fulfilled his promise, again refusing to accept any money for his gift.

This was my introduction to Tabari, an Arab Moslem businessman from East Jerusalem. I learned that, among other things, he was a gourmet chef whose family owned a restaurant. He had learned the trade from his father, a renowned chef who had prepared meals for King Hussein and other dignitaries.

Over the following year, I purchased many necklaces from Tabari, giving them to partners supporting our ministries in the Middle East.

In October 1982, we made plans to meet in the Jerusalem Hilton hotel where I would reimburse Tabari for the necklaces he had mailed to my office at Christian Retreat in Bradenton, Florida.

Spotting the familiar smile, I motioned Tabari over to a seating area in the lobby. He seemed genuinely glad to see me, and we chatted comfortably as we sipped our Cokes.

Then began a conversation that would impact our lives forever.

"I like you...you are different," Tabari said. "Why are you different?"

"Because I am a Christian," I replied. "Do you know what a Christian is?"

"Yes, I'm Christian," he replied.

"No, you told me earlier that you are Arab and Moslem," I said.

"Yes, I'm Moslem...I like everybody!"

Pressing further, I asked him, "Have you ever heard of a born-again Christian?"

"No, what is a born-again Christian?"

I explained that to be a born-again Christian is quite different than being only Christian. Many people have religion; some belong to the Buddhist religion, some are Moslem, some Christian. Many people in the world have religion and call themselves Christians.

I once was like that, I told him. Born into a Mennonite family, I was raised in a very religious home and faithfully attended church. But my life didn't change...I didn't become *different*, until I became a *born-again* Christian.

Staring intently at me, Tabari asked, "May I be a man of peace like you?"

"Yes," I replied. "You can be a man of peace."

"No, I mean can I become like you say, *born again*?"

"Yes, of course you can become born again," I said.

Becoming even more insistent, he burst out, "No, I mean, *can you do it to me now?*"

I suddenly realized that this young Arab man was serious. "Allow me some time," I said, "and I will explain how you can be born again."

For the next hour, I relayed the simple gospel message and the plan of salvation. Then Tabari grasped my hands across the table and repeated the sinner's prayer, confessing Jesus Christ as His Lord, acknowledging that God could have a son, and that Jesus Christ shed his blood so true peace could affect his heart and cause him to walk with God in this world.

Thus, this Arab Moslem man was born into the Kingdom of God.

"I feel so different," he exclaimed, his face aglow.

"What do you feel?" I asked.

"I feel so light. I feel peace. I feel so good!"

"Your spirit is being quickened by the Holy Spirit of God," I replied, "and you are becoming born again."

That encounter set in motion a miraculous series of events that are unfolding still...a phenomenon that has left us awed and humbled as we've seen God open doors for us among some of the most hard-to-reach people in the world: the Moslems.

Chapter Two

A Prophetic New Beginning

I had always known about the Jews. They were the Strauss boys who lived down the block. As youngsters growing up in the suburban outskirts of Philadelphia, my two brothers and I were taught not to pick on anyone—not even Jews. Even if all the other guys did.

In those World War II days, we heard the terrible tales of Jewish persecution in German concentration camps. Well, if anyone was going to be oppressed, we were glad it was the Jews and not Christians or Mennonites. After all, weren't the Jews the ones who crucified Jesus? Perhaps it was God's punishment.

As for Arabs, well, I never thought much about them. I didn't know any personally. Camels, sand dunes, oil wells, Arabs—they were all quite foreign to me and my life.

In fact, I gave less thought to them than I did to the Jews. What had Arabs ever done for us Christians? At least the Jews gave us Jesus and the Bible.

I had heard in Sunday school the story of Abraham and Hagar in Genesis 21, how Ishmael had been conceived and cast out. Although the Jews were "God's chosen people," the Arabs had nothing to do with God's blessing, I thought.

Through the years, as I studied my Bible further, I began to see the common heritage we as Christian and Jew shared. I also began to note how God's dealing with Israel and the Jews related to ancient Bible prophecy—prophecy that was being fulfilled in this day. It began to dawn on me that perhaps His people and His land were the world's "time clock" by which we could recognize end-time events leading to Christ's return.

Israel's astounding victory in 1967 during the Six-Day War further piqued my interest and sent me searching through the Scriptures. Did God still have a special love for this land? Did He have a plan that He was going to fulfill?

In 1970, Beulah and I took our first trip to Israel. Visiting the holy sites and walking where Jesus walked was an unforgettable experience. But it wasn't until September 1980, ten years and many visits later, that my eyes were opened...dramatically.

That was the year the International Christian Embassy, Jerusalem (ICEJ) was established. At a time when, as a sign of protest, many nations from around the world pulled their embassies out of the Holy City, a small band of Christians displayed their love for Israel by firmly planting their roots in Jerusalem. Called the Almond Branch, which means "bridge," they lived in Israel as Israeli citizens, and had been praying for the day when they could tell the Jews that the Jewish people, and the land of Israel, are loved by Christians around the world.

In September 1980, Israel's government, under the leadership of Prime Minister Menachem Begin, accepted the Christian community. For the first time in its history, Israel established official dialogue with them and gave the Christians the right to have an embassy in Jerusalem.

When the United Nations and the world abandoned Israel, the door was opened for God's army, the Church, the Body of Christ—Jesus—to come forth.

Our tour group that was there at the time witnessed this small, yet significant, beginning. They also witnessed an event that would change the direction of my life.

We were at the Diplomat Hotel. Jan Willem Van der Hoeven, the former keeper of the Garden Tomb and one of the founders of the ICEJ, had finished explaining to us the purpose and vision of the new embassy. Then he placed his hands on my head and gave forth a powerful prophecy.

"You will be powerfully used of God throughout the United States and North America to teach the relationship between Christians and Jews...you will be a messenger who is used to enlighten Christians about their responsibility to the Jews...God will take you to the cities, to the churches, and you will have an understanding and clearly explain to Christians why they should love this land and focus their eyes upon the people of this land...."

As Brother Van der Hoeven spoke those words, I thought he must have gotten the wrong man. Sure, I loved coming to Israel and touring the land, but I certainly didn't feel *that* strongly about the Jews. I was a Bible teacher who loved expounding on the Kingdom of God, enlightening Christians about who they were in Christ and how they could be effective in their faith.

Yet I had always respected this outspoken and charismatic Dutchman as a true prophet of God. So I tucked his words on a shelf in my mind. Perhaps I would understand later.

The following year our tour coincided with the first ICEJ Christian celebration of the Feast of Tabernacles in Jerusalem. As I listened to the teachings, my eyes began to open and a fire began to burn within me. It all began to fall into place. Yes, we Christians had a mission to accomplish. We had a responsibility to the Jews, to Israel, to the land. They all played a crucial part in the fulfillment of Bible prophecy and God's end-time plan.

I came home from that trip feeling as though I had become born again—again!

My ministry and life has never been the same.

Chapter Three

Threatened by Terrorists

In 1983, the year following his conversion, Tabari took me home to meet his family in East Jerusalem.

"My family wants to meet your family...please, you must visit my home and have a meal with us," he said.

Like most Arab families in the Middle East, his was a large one. They lived—several generations together—in a small, sparsely-furnished home with high ceilings and bare floors.

We were informed that Tabari's father would not be present as he was on a pilgrimage to Mecca, Islam's holiest place. However, Tabari's mother, dressed in typical Arab garb, greeted us warmly at the door. The household bustled with activity as a lavish feast, prepared by Tabari and his brother, was spread out for us.

We had never seen such an array of food! It was a banquet fit for a king, and after we finally convinced our hosts that we could eat no more, it seemed as though we had barely touched what was there. Then, before we left, we were given beautiful gifts to remember our visit. How could we ever forget!

That was our first taste of Arab hospitality, and it was just the beginning.

Another year Tabari and his family prepared a lovely meal for all 80 of our tour members. With each visit, relationships were built and trust earned. I learned later that this was the most effective way to reach the Arab Moslem community. It was a slow process, but if we were patient, it would eventually reap rewards and the gospel would be received.

As I visited with Tabari's family following this great banquet feast, they asked me, "Will you consider coming to live with us and teaching us about God?"

"We are many," Tabari said. "We are thousands of people...we are villages and cities. Our family has lived in the Galilee region for more than 500 years. Please come and be our holy man. We will give you a house to live in and furnish it, and also put food in the refrigerator."

Could they really be serious? Returning home, I told Beulah, "I must come to Israel alone and search out this invitation."

In the fall of 1986, I drove up the Jordan Valley from Jerusalem to Tiberius with Tabari, his brother and his mother.

I was introduced to brothers, sisters, uncles, aunts, cousins, nieces and nephews—all of them related somehow to this family. With the Arabs' customary large families of 10 or 14 children, it didn't take many generations to produce an entire village!

Everywhere we went, from house to house, we were invited inside for sweets or fruit and thick, black coffee. I was overwhelmed. I had never seen this side of Israel before.

Deep inside, I began to realize that this was the beginning of something big. God was opening a door that many people thought was impossible to penetrate. Reaching Arab Moslems with the gospel message of Jesus Christ was a task at which few had succeeded, even after many years of intense missionary work.

Since my involvement with Gospel Crusade in 1955, we had pioneered many mission outreaches throughout the world. Thousands of churches and many schools, orphanages and Bible Institutes had been planted in Haiti, the Philippines, Honduras and many other countries. Beulah and I and our four children had spent much time on foreign soil, establishing missionary works and bringing food, clothing, Bibles and medical supplies to the needy.

Ever since the age of nine, I had felt the call to be a missionary, and God had wonderfully fulfilled that call in my life.

But now, when approaching 60, I knew God was sending me on a divine mission unlike any other I had undertaken. I could hardly contain my excitement.

"Beulah, I must go back," I told my wife upon my return to our home at Christian Retreat in Florida. "And we need to go together the next time."

With our children all grown and our oldest son, Phil, managing Christian Retreat and the Gospel Crusade ministry, my wife and I now felt free to travel together.

The following spring, in May 1987, we made plans to journey back to Israel and spend some time in the homes of our new-found friends. We were not aware, until we arrived, that our visit coincided with Ramadan, the annual holy month during which Moslems fast and pray.

We had been warned by some people that it was dangerous to go into Moslem communities, especially during this month. Although most are peace-loving, some fanatical Moslems hate Christians and seek to harm them. Indeed, we discovered firsthand that this was true.

The winter months had blessed Israel with precious rain, and her northern hills and mountains were blanketed in spring green. Splashes of red, purple and yellow wildflowers interrupted the tender green landscape. What a contrast to the drab, dry browns of late summer and fall!

We were to spend a few days with the family of Samir, a cousin of Tabari, in a village a stone's throw away from the Sea of Galilee.

Samir's family and neighbors eyed us curiously as we brought our suitcases into the house. Obviously, this bit of Israel was not on the tourist circuit.

The first night was uneventful and we slept comfortably, though we were jarred awake by the piercing, amplified calls to early morning prayer by the Moslem priest in the nearby mosque:

"La ilaha ill Allah,
Muhammad rasoolullah!"

"There is no God but Allah:
And Mohammed is the Prophet of God."

On the second day of our stay, our Arab brothers, eager to introduce us to more family members, took us for a drive. Upon arriving back in the village late that afternoon, we found Samir's family visibly disturbed.

Apparently a group of fanatical Moslems from a neighboring village had been sent by their leaders to warn the family that the visiting American couple must leave the village immediately or Samir's family and village would suffer dire consequences.

"We must come together tonight and pray," our Christian Arab brothers told us. So that evening seven very sober-faced people gathered to seek the Lord about this threat of violence.

I shared with them some Scriptures about persecution, and how the Bible instructs us to deal with an enemy. "They will come back again tomorrow," I said, "but don't argue. Say 'yes' to as many of their statements as possible."

Directing them to their Bibles, I read Matthew 5:25a: "Agree with thine adversary quickly, whiles thou art in the way with him."

"If the terrorists push you or dare to strike you," I said, "what would Jesus do?" Referring to the Sermon on the Mount, I read, "...whosoever shall smite thee on thy right cheek, turn to him the other also" (Matt. 5:39). I slapped each of my cheeks to demonstrate this.

Sa'id, a friend of Tabari's, suddenly got the point. "Yes," he said with excitement, "and if they kill us, it will be finished, then we will go to Heaven and be with Jesus!"

"No, Sa'id," I replied quickly, smiling, "God doesn't want you in Heaven yet. You have a work to do here. And don't forget, God can change their hearts. We will join our hands tonight and pray that God will change their minds and they will not harm us."

That night before we went to bed, we prayed fervently, asking for God's protection and direction. Beulah and I settled into our bed, trying not to think about what might be lurking in the darkness. We slept, undisturbed, and woke to another day of visiting relatives and friends.

We could not have imagined, however, the surprise that awaited us upon our return to the village that afternoon.

We were told that the leader of the terrorist gang had come to the house, full of apologies, exclaiming that Allah had not let him rest.

"I could not sleep all night," he exclaimed. "Allah kept me awake, tossing and turning because of what I said about the American couple. Please accept my apology, so that Allah will let me rest! It is okay, the American couple can stay in the village."

We rejoiced at God's swift answer to our prayers. But that was not the end. The next day he came back again, saying that all day his mind had been troubled with horrible thoughts and he had not slept another entire night. He wanted to apologize all over again so Allah would let him rest!

Nine months later we learned that this man separated himself from the enemy camp and became a friend to the believers in that village.

For two weeks Beulah and I circulated among these people, fellowshipping and planting seeds of the gospel message. At night in different homes, they gathered around us asking questions and listening eagerly to what we had to say.

It was during this time, while sharing with a group of people in one of the homes, that we heard of the first miraculous visitation.

Chapter Four

Fatima's Vision

Twilight had gently descended upon the land of the Bible that Sunday evening, and stars were beginning to pierce the heavenly canopy of darkening blue as Beulah and I visited in a house packed with Tabari's relatives. Squeezed tightly together on the couches and overflowing onto the floor, they listened intently as we shared why we had come to their community.

Tabari interpreted my words into Arabic.

"When I met Tabari in 1981, I wasn't attempting to convert him to Christianity," I said. "He asked me questions and then he said, 'I wish I could be like you.'

"I told him I was born again. That's why I am here now, because you invited me to come. And you want me to tell you what I know about God." I then proceeded to explain how to be born again.

Asking them to pray with me (something I knew they had never done before), I said, "I will pray first and then we will pray together. When we pray we just bow our heads and close our eyes. We think upon God. God is a Spirit and we think upon Him.

"I will pray now and I want everybody to be quiet and listen," I said, careful to keep my instructions simple.

Self-consciously glancing at one another before bowing their heads, they followed my instructions like little children. We prayed the sinner's prayer together, and I believe that everyone in the room, both adults and young people, received Christ into their hearts.

Then something amazing happened.

One of the women began to tremble. Her name was Fatima, meaning "daughter of Mohammed." When we inquired as to what was wrong, she began telling us about a vision she had seen a year ago during this same time, Ramadan, the Moslem holy month of fasting and prayer.

"It happened during the daytime," she explained, "so I know I was not dreaming."

In this vision, she said, she saw three women in white coming toward her, along with three priests dressed in black. A man was lying on the ground, a man she identified as Jesus. One of the priests touched Him on His thigh, another priest touched Jesus on the shoulder, and He stood up and began to walk toward her.

Then somehow He became a baby, and Fatima found herself holding Him in her arms. As she cuddled the baby, the Christ-child vomited. She said "it poured out of his mouth." One of the priests quickly said, "Don't let it fall to the ground but catch it, hold it and now rub it between your hands."

Fatima's face lit up as she exclaimed, "Suddenly, while rubbing this substance in my hands, a brilliant light overwhelmed my hands, my body trembled, and the whole room burst ablaze with this exceedingly bright light!"

In the days following, she said, she often thought of this strange experience, sometimes even finding herself holding her hands in the position of cuddling the Christ-child. She would tremble and ponder its meaning.

What did it mean? she wondered. When she could no longer stand the suspense, she determined to seek out an explanation.

Since the people she saw in the vision appeared to be Christian Catholics, she went to a Greek Orthodox (Catholic) church to ask a priest if he could tell her the meaning of this vision.

The priest, however, could only say that what had happened to her was something good, and that during the next Ramadan a holy man and a companion would come to her village and explain the meaning of the vision.

Beulah and I rejoiced as we listened to this incredible story. At first we had been somewhat embarrassed that we had unknowingly scheduled our visit during Ramadan, as many Moslems customarily fasted until evening. Nevertheless, as their guests, we were politely offered food, and some of them forsook their religious tradition in favor of Arab hospitality and ate along with us.

Now we realized that God had sovereignly led us here at this time. The hour had come for God's visitation to the hundreds of thousands of the sons of Ishmael in the Middle East.

I asked Beulah to explain the meaning of Fatima's vision, as I knew she understood it as well as I did. Choosing her words carefully, she told them that the substance coming from the mouth of Jesus is the *life* that God promises to those who believe that Jesus is God's Son.

As believers, she said, we are lights in this world. This light illuminates the meaning of the Holy Book, the Bible, to us. The light is the life of the Holy Spirit of God, making each one of us holy people (John 8:12).

The room was silent as Beulah finished her explanation. Yet as I looked around at the faces, I knew they had understood, and we all rejoiced at the miracle God had worked in our midst.

It was already 10:15 p.m., but the evening had not ended. There was another houseful of Arab Moslem friends, about six doors away, who wished to hear what we had to say. There had not been room for them in the first house.

So we walked to our next assignment and spoke till nearly midnight. Fatima went along to repeat her part of the story. These people, mostly youth, also prayed the sinner's prayer and opened their hearts to receive our Lord and Savior.

"Are you the first born-again Christian who has come to the world?" asked one young man.

"No," I told him emphatically, "there have been millions of people born again since Jesus died on the cross!"

"How come we never heard about being born again until now?" he persisted.

"Because *now is your time,*" I replied. "*God is visiting your people now!*"

Chapter Five

"We Can Live With the Jews"

Although overjoyed at the miraculous conversions we were seeing, I also began to realize that these young leaders needed discipling and Bible training. So earlier that year, in March 1987, we had arranged for Tabari and his cousin, Samir, to attend our Institute of Ministry at Christian Retreat in Florida.

Our form of worship was entirely foreign to them. However, they were soon shouting "Praise the Lord!" along with their new-found brothers and sisters and enjoying the warmth of Christian fellowship.

During this time, the two young men expressed their desire for water baptism. Rejoicing at their decision to fully commit themselves to Jesus, I immersed them in the Manatee River.

To my astonishment, Tabari immediately dropped himself back into the water, immersing himself two more times.

"Why did you do that?" I asked, perplexed.

"I must have the blessing of Israel," he replied. "I choose to be immersed three times in order to be blessed by the God of Abraham, Isaac and Jacob."

"You, an Arab Moslem, now receiving the blessing of a Jew...!" I responded in amazement. "Praise the Lord!"

Before returning to Jerusalem, Tabari stated that the next time I visited Israel, he would introduce me to the leader of the majority of Arab Moslems on the West Bank.

"You are a friend to Yassir Arafat?" I asked.

"No, Arafat is not the majority leader of West Bank Arabs," he replied. "He is a terrorist who represents the PLO (Palestine Liberation Organization), but his people are not the majority. Mr. Jameel is the majority leader of peace-loving Arabs, and he and I are close friends."

He had succeeded in arousing my curiosity!

Tabari continued, saying, "When I introduce you to my friend, Mr. Jameel...he will like you! When you know he likes you, you invite him to come to Christian Retreat, Florida. He will come! When he comes, he will then also understand about Jesus like me, and he will invite you to come to West Bank and Gaza Strip Arab Moslem villages to teach them about Jesus."

True to his word, Tabari introduced us to this high-ranking official, Mr. Jameel, during our visit in May. A handsome, forty-ish man with a thick shock of dark hair streaked with silver, he exuded an air of authority.

Like most Americans, I had thought all Arabs in Israel were followers of the leftist Yassir Arafat, whose goal was to push the Jewish people into the Mediterranean Sea and take the land of Israel away from them. However, I learned that most of the 400,000 Arab Moslems in West Bank territories are content with their present conditions and do not support the PLO philosophy.

Mr. Jameel at that time was mayor of an Arab village and chairman of the Village Leagues, an organization of 43 Arab Moslem villages in league with Jewish Israel, located on the West Bank and Gaza Strip. Jameel was highly respected and trusted by both Arabs and Jewish government leaders in the Knesset, the parliament of Israel.

"Most Arabs in Israel are praying for peace and the stability of the Israeli government," he explained, as we toured in his luxurious Mercedes Benz. "We can live with the Jews! We are cousins...we have the same father, Abraham." He estimated that 70 percent of the Arab Moslems on the West Bank agree with his peace philosophy, while the remaining 30 percent are under the leadership and influence of the PLO.

"What have they ever done for us?" he exclaimed. "All they offer is terrorism, killings and unrest. Do they pave any streets for us? No. Did they ever build any schools for us? No...only the Jewish Israel has paved streets and built schools and clinics in our villages."

We were invited to be Jameel's guests at a sumptuous Eastern banquet at his friend's house in Ramallah, an Arab city on the West Bank. There, in a large, lovely home, we met two other mayors and a number of businessmen and educators. Tabari told us that these were very wealthy men.

Sitting on colorful mats on the floor, Beulah and I received a lesson in ancient Bedouin tradition as we learned to eat with our fingers. (We noted that the guests had left their shoes at the door and carefully washed their hands before eating.) They all dipped into a large steaming tray of spiced rice and lamb, much as Abraham and Moses must have done in Bible days. Baskets of freshly baked pita bread and plates filled with a variety of salads surrounded the main course.

Just before we began to eat, Jameel took a morsel of the meat and placed it into my mouth with his fingers. He explained that this was their way of showing we were his honored guests. During the banquet, at prayer time, some of these men knelt down, with face on the floor and body positioned toward Mecca.

The next day Jameel drove us to Hebron and other villages on the West Bank, introducing us to mayors and councilmen. At one of the villages I had the privilege of playing a song on my harmonica. The people clapped their hands, delighted at this joyful music so foreign to their own. They told me that, as far as they could remember, I was the first American to enter into some of these Moslem villages, the area where Abraham, Isaac and Jacob lived and worshiped God in Bible days.

We gathered for dinner again that evening in Jameel's village, with approximately 50 of his relatives, friends and town leaders. Again we sat on the floor, propped up on pillows while we awkwardly attempted to imitate our hosts' table manners. Feeling a little silly at first, we soon learned to ball up the rice in our fist, then, with a thumb, pop the tasty rice ball into our mouth.

Later, on the roof of the house, I spoke through an interpreter to a large crowd of men. I was welcome to come back again, they told me, and, in fact, could my wife and I stay for another three days...or at least overnight?

Beulah and I were beginning to learn that hospitality is taken very seriously by the Arabs. An old tradition requires them to welcome a stranger into their home for up to three days before even asking his name or intentions. When their forefathers wandered as nomads in the harsh desert, one's life might depend on the food and shelter offered by the Bedouins.

As we departed from his home, Jameel presented us with a beautiful "peace plate," a plate decorated with various symbols and words for peace in Arabic, English and Hebrew. This, he said, represented evidence of our working together to seek God's blessing with His peace upon the earth, particularly in the Middle East.

Honored by this gesture, I responded with an invitation.

"Will you come to America as my guest?" I asked. "Yes, Mr. Gerald, I would like that," Jameel replied.

At that moment, I recalled how Tabari spoke to me while he was in Florida, how this man would like me and that if I invited him to Christian Retreat, "He will come!"

As we traveled home from the Hebron region that night, the four of us—Tabari, Samir, Beulah and I—sang and rejoiced. Our praises echoed over the Judean hills and the glory of God overwhelmed us as we realized that God was doing a new thing to bring peace among Jews, Arabs and Christians in the Middle East.

Jameel came to Christian Retreat as our guest in August 1987. Tabari accompanied him. Over the first several days, I listened as Jameel talked politics and he listened as I talked about Jesus.

On the second day of his visit, he confronted me.

"Mr. Gerald, on television I see people being prayed for and they say that now they are healed. Do you believe like this? Does your religion also believe that way?"

"Yes," I replied. "We believe that God can heal our bodies."

"You do believe this?" he persisted.

"Yes, of course we do," I answered.

At that, Jameel turned slowly around, pointed toward his lower back and said, "Please. Put your hands here and pray."

He didn't need to ask twice. I laid my hands on his back and prayed fervently, asking God to perform a miracle of healing.

As I said "Amen," Jameel exclaimed, "It's gone! No more pain! It's totally gone!"

Now the door was wide open. From that time on, it was easy to teach him from the Bible and explain how Jesus was more than a holy teacher and prophet.

The following day, I received a phone call from Israel. On the line was a man who introduced himself as Secretary and Chairman of the Likud Party in Israel's Knesset.

"I'm calling to inform you that this Arab gentleman, Jameel, is a very important man," the caller said. "He could be our most viable man of the West Bank to enable Jewish Israel and Arab Moslems to negotiate a peace solution.

"Take very good care of this man, introduce him to your people of America, to the cities. Take him to Washington, D.C. and introduce him to your congressmen and senators."

Over the next few weeks, we arranged meetings with several government officials in major cities and interviews with the news media.

"Only God can help us," Jameel said in one interview. "We all believe in God; therefore, we can come together to negotiate...You are people of the Book; we are people of the Book. The Koran tells us that God is one; you believe that God is one. There is no difference. Where God is, there is peace, and without God there cannot be any peace."

We had devotions from the Bible every day that we were together. Several times he told me, "Gerald, I feel that God has brought you into my life to be a mediator for peace in my country.

"The moment that I first saw you, I felt something leap within me, like something turned upside down and God showed me that you were the man He could use to help us bring the peace."

Meanwhile, Jameel's activities in America had not gone unnoticed in the Middle East. Radio broadcasts from Syria were breathing out threats against him, saying that he was a traitor to the Palestinian cause and promising death to him upon his return. These reports came to us from his secretaries whom he would contact in one of his six offices in Israel.

He had told us that Arafat's PLO had attempted to assassinate him three times. I personally saw the bullet-riddled wall of his home, mute evidence of one of the attacks.

But he was not afraid. "Allah gives the life," Jameel said. "I enjoy the life that Allah gives, until it is taken away. I could not be a leader if I were to be afraid. If they take my life, another one will step forward to take my place. Nothing will stand in the way of the peace that God wills."

I have been criticized for befriending an Arab Moslem. Some believe that the man should have become a Christian before I began working with him.

However, I believe that God orders the steps of a righteous man. God used people in Bible times, and He uses them today. Only eternity will know how Jameel was influenced by those in our Christian Retreat community and by the enthusiastic worship services—the first he ever experienced.

"I wish my people to be happy like your people," he remarked wistfully. "Please come and help our people to know God like you know God."

Chapter Six

Paying the Price

Painted by a harvest moon, the Sea of Galilee shimmered with a coat of silver. The seaside city of Tiberius was hushed as Jewish families observed Shabbat, the Sabbath, in their homes.

Inside the vacant discothèque of our hotel, Sa'id was seated facing our tour group of 32 people. His angular face serious, the slightly built young Arab man fidgeted, appearing uncomfortable in the luxurious setting.

He leaned forward, elbows resting on his knees, hands clasped, his piercing eyes demanding our attention.

"Please take a message back to America," he pleaded. "It's not true what your media is telling you. We Palestinians don't want the PLO...we have been killed by the millions under Arab rule. We want to live in peace, and we have seen that the Jews are better rulers.

"We don't want Arafat. If a state of Palestine happens, it will be bad for everyone!"

Sa'id, 38, who lives on the Israeli-occupied West Bank, risked his life with those words.

He said that his beliefs are shared by most of the Palestinians living in that land. But few dare to speak openly, fearful of being labeled a "traitor" and being brutally executed by PLO terrorists.

"I have seen with my own eyes what happens to someone who says they don't want the PLO," he said. "I have seen a man whose eyes were pulled out, and his liver cut out."

More often their shops and homes are fire-bombed, their families terrorized.

News reports are one-sided, he said. Israeli soldiers are depicted as ruthless aggressors, beating on helpless Arab men, women and children. In reality, the soldiers exercise considerable restraint, he said.

"There are a lot of cases where soldiers could kill all they want, but they don't."

He told of witnessing "blood streaming down a Jewish woman's face as stones are thrown through her car windows." These incidents go untold by the media, he said.

We call Sa'id the "Peter" of our group of believers. I imagine he is as outspoken, opinionated and charismatic as the Peter of Bible days.

Like Tabari, Sa'id had been a chef and maître d' of some of the larger hotels in Jerusalem. Unlike most of the other Arabs in our fold, he is a Palestinian from the Hebron region, an area that was (and still is, as of this writing) a politically volatile region, with much tension and many outbreaks of violence.

Although Tabari and other Arab Moslems in the Galilee region are officially Israeli citizens, those who live in Sa'id's community are considered Jordanians and do not enjoy all the privileges of Israeli citizenship. They are under the jurisdiction, however, of the Israeli army and their municipalities are serviced by the Israeli government.

A PLO-enforced strike, now in its fifth year, has deprived many Arabs of their livelihoods, impoverished them, and forced their children into the streets. Schools may be closed for months, and those fortunate enough to find a school to attend must pay a price.

"If you want to go to school you have to throw stones," Sa'id said.

Young boys are taught to pack stones into their schoolbags—stones to throw at Israeli soldiers.

"They're being taught to hate the Israelis," he said. "They're even going against what is written in the Koran."

When possible, Sa'id confides that he discreetly pulls the children aside and reasons with them.

Since becoming born again through the witness of his long-time friend, Tabari, Sa'id has become fearless in his zeal for the Lord. Now sharing leadership of our work in Israel, he conducts nightly clandestine meetings for hundreds of new believers in the Hebron region. They study the Bible by the flickering light of a kerosene lamp.

"Many times we do not know where our next meal is coming from," he said. "But it doesn't matter. What I suffer for the Lord is nothing compared to what Jesus did for me. He went to the cross and died, gave His life for me...."

Raised in a strict Moslem family, Sa'id does not take his conversion lightly. The Koran dictates that Moslems who convert to Christianity must be put to death immediately—no trial, no mercy.

Even as a baby Christian, Sa'id tasted the meaning of sacrifice. His wife left their home, saying she could not live with an infidel (one who departed from the Moslem faith) and went to live with her parents in Jordan.

His mother, who had made a pilgrimage to Mecca, was extremely distressed by her son's new commitment. They used to "fight and argue," Sa'id said, and finally his mother ordered him out of the house—until one night when a man in white came to her in a vision. He sat beside her and said, "Leave your son alone to do what he is doing. He is saying the Truth."

At 2 a.m. she woke Sa'id and told him that God had visited her, saying her son was chosen to fulfill a special mission as peacemaker in Israel. They wept and prayed together. "Son, I must follow you as you follow God," she exclaimed.

Some months later, Sa'id's prayers were answered when his wife and two young daughters returned home. "I don't care what has happened," his wife told him. "All I want is you and the Lord." She now shares her husband's vision of bringing peace to their land, and has her own ministry among the Moslem women in their community.

Their life is not easy.

One night around 2 a.m., Sa'id felt God impressing him to get up and go over to the building where they had been holding Bible studies. He considered this idea with caution as there was a curfew, and if he was caught, he could have suffered serious consequences.

Arriving at the building, he saw fire shooting from the window. A man's body lay on the ground near the entrance. Quickly dousing the flames, which were created by a gasoline molotov-style bomb that had been thrown into the window, Sa'id managed to extinguish the fire.

Afterwards he dragged the unconscious man to his home, and with his wife's help, bound up the man's wounds. As the man regained consciousness, he asked in astonishment, "Why are you helping me? I tried to burn your building...!"

"I am doing this because I love you," Sa'id told him. "And God loves you."

God touched the man's heart through Sa'id's act of mercy, and he accepted Christ. Later his wife and seven children also became dedicated workers in this growing church.

Tragically, this same man some eight months after his conversion was lured outside his house by former Islamic companions and brutally slashed to pieces with knives. Offered as a sacrifice to Allah, he was our second martyr. His wife was stabbed six times with deep wounds, but survived. Pray for Nadia and her seven children.

Our first martyr, a fine young 27-year-old man, also from that region, was stabbed to death in front of his young 21-year-old wife and three sons. Because he had become a follower of the Messiah, Jesus, he was considered an infidel by these religious, fundamental Moslems.

Sa'id's own family would not escape the cruelty of fanatical Islam.

After giving birth to two lovely daughters, Sa'id and his wife were delighted when God blessed them with a son. They honored me by naming him "Gerald," even though they knew it was against Islamic religious rules to give a child a non-Moslem name.

Ten days after Baby Gerald was born, a couple came to visit Sa'id's home. Holding the infant, the Moslem man asked the mother, "What did you name your child?"

"His name is Gerald," she answered.

"What is that?" he asked.

As Sa'id's wife began to explain to them our friendship, the Moslem man suddenly and deliberately slammed the infant on the concrete floor in an attempt to kill him.

Baby Gerald was severely injured. His body was crushed internally, he was blinded in one eye, and his heart and liver were jolted out of position. He cried constantly. Doctors gave him less than a year to live.

We began praying, many churches in America joining with us, and God gave Sa'id's child a miracle. It came through my wife, Beulah. She was obedient to a prophetic word that came to her in 1990 while she was in a service at Christian Retreat. When she next went to Israel, she was to hold Baby Gerald in her arms and he would be healed.

She did exactly that. The miracle, verified by doctors, came to pass. Baby Gerald slept peacefully through the night for the first time in his life.

Five months later, however, we were shocked to receive word that Baby Gerald was dead.

Apparently someone had secretly poisoned the baby's milk, sending him into convulsions and resulting in a violent death.

Though shaken to the core by their agonizing loss, Sa'id and his wife refused to become bitter, and clung to their faith in Jesus. God rewarded them not long after with another son, whom they named Samuel.

But the story does not end there.

Chapter Seven

The Most Amazing Conversions

I had just finished shaving early one morning in January 1991 when the phone rang. On the other end was Sa'id's voice, calling me from Israel. The story he told us left Beulah and I staring at one another in amazement....

A high Islamic official had been wounded in a skirmish with the Israeli soldiers on the West Bank. While he recuperated at his home, Sa'id's wife, Laura, and her mother-in-law called on him, attempting to console him. This was a customary practice in the Moslem community.

As they were visiting, the man related the details of how his arm and leg had been wounded.

"Tomorrow they're going to amputate my arm because of blood poisoning," he told them.

Laura immediately felt impressed to pray for his recovery.

"Please, let me pray for you," she said.

The man laughed. "What good can prayer do for me now?" Laura persisted. "Let me pray for you." Again he laughed, but then agreed to humor her. "I guess your prayers wouldn't hurt," he said.

She courageously reached out to touch his wounded arm and he let out a cry. As she laid her hands on him and began to pray he felt the power of God surge through his body. The Moslem official's arm was instantly healed!

He fell on his knees, and crying aloud began kissing her feet. "I'm not worthy. I'm not worthy. You don't understand. Why are you so good to me?"

He continued to repeat those words, "I'm not worthy..."

At Laura's puzzled expression, the man trembled as he began to explain.

"I am the man who is responsible for killing your child," he confessed. "I gave the orders to send the man and woman to your house and slam your baby to the floor to kill your son. Why are you nice to me, praying for me to be healed when I have been so wicked to you?"

He looked across the room and pointed to his wife.

"This is my wife sitting over there. I gave her the poison and ordered her to go to your house and place the poison in your baby's food with the intent to kill your child."

He was weaping even more uncontrollably now. "How can you be so good to me? What must I do? What must I do?"

Sa'id's wife, shocked, but understanding the Islamic law that is according to Moses—an eye for an eye and tooth for a tooth—calmly said, "I gave a life, my only son. You said your wife put the poison in the milk. She is a life, an adult life..."

As she spoke, the official's wife's skin turned yellow. Suddenly, she collapsed to the floor and died.

Her husband began to scream. "Pray, pray! I see flames of fire! She is being eaten by snakes in hell!" The man was given a vision of his wife slipping into hell's fire.

Through this experience, the official had a sovereign revelation of Jesus Christ and cried, "I must know God and Jesus as you know Him...I will serve you and your people."

Later this same man revealed five photos he had of me, and showed documents that were written and signed for my execution the previous year.

I remembered the event well. It was in March 1990, and I had visited that region in spite of warnings to stay away because of political tensions and terrorist activity. The night I was being driven into the village, God sovereignly caused a torrential rain that forced the terrorist gang indoors as my auto passed by.

The man confessed to other incidents of violence, of killing and beating believers. Now he also is a believer, thanks to the fervent prayers of the persecuted church on the West Bank!

Naturally, word of this phenomenon spread. The woman who had died was quite young, the mother of two small children. Curious as to what caused her untimely demise, her family insisted on an autopsy. However, specialists could find no disease, no germs of any kind. They finally determined it to be a natural death.

I questioned Sa'id about the couple who had actually slammed Baby Gerald to the floor. Whatever happened to them?

"I don't know their names," he said. "I could never get any information about that couple, and we never heard anything further from any source."

"Now that the official who was responsible for sending them is saved, does he know who they are?" I asked.

"Yes," Sa'id replied, "he knows who they are. They are friends of his, but he does not want to divulge their name or get them in any trouble."

Then, in December 1991, Sa'id's wife telephoned him in America while he was visiting us and told the most incredible story.

She said that she had been asked to pray for a woman dying of cancer. She later learned that the woman was the wife of the man who had slammed Baby Gerald to the floor. Only under much pressure had the husband, a Moslem sheik, permitted Laura, a Christian woman, to come to his house and pray for his dying wife.

Odeh was a man filled with hate for Christians. A leader in an Islamic mosque in that region, he had exclaimed, "If you bring her [Laura] into my house, I do not want to meet her. I will stay in a separate room, because I hate Christians."

His wife had already been discharged from the hospital and sent home to die. Her entire right side was lifeless, and there was no hope of recovery.

Laying her hands upon the dying woman, Laura prayed earnestly. When she prayed, the sick woman let out a scream as a strong surge of the power of God went through her body. She was miraculously healed! Straightening her once-paralyzed legs, she stepped out of bed and began to walk.

Even though she knew her husband hated Christians, she took Laura's arm and walked into the man's room. He couldn't believe his eyes! Here was his wife, who only moments earlier had been nearly dead, happily standing before him, completely healed. Beside her stood the Christian woman.

In shock, his twisted mind could think of only one thing: suicide. Grabbing a huge butcher knife, he began to scream, "I must die!" He raised the knife high, poised to stab himself.

In that instant, Laura shouted, "*Stop*, in the name of Jesus!"

The man froze, and then crashed to the floor. After appearing unconscious for about ten minutes, he slowly emerged from his trancelike state and, with his wife, that day became a believer in the Messiah, Jesus Christ.

Sealing his pledge, he stated that when his wife had another baby son, his name would be Gerald.

Several months later, I was privileged to meet this man and woman. I learned that he had renamed his youngest son "Gerald." He and his five children are now part of our team in this Palestinian West Bank community.

God will do what He must do, and no man can stop it.

Chapter Eight

Miracle in Cana

"The pastor of the church in Cana of Galilee wants to meet you," Tabari told me in October 1989.

"What do you mean, 'church in Cana'?" I asked, puzzled. "I have not been to Cana. How could we have a church there?"

I knew that Cana, near Nazareth, is populated primarily by the fanatical fringe of the Islamic people, and it often contains an undercurrent of hostility. A visit to certain parts of that village could be risky...and an Arab Moslem professing Christ could be signing his death warrant.

Curious, I decided to take our tour group that year along with me to visit this new church. Driving into the village, our bus inched through narrow, winding streets, ascended a hill and finally stopped next to a tree-encircled courtyard. Next to the courtyard was a house with many people standing outside.

Stepping off the bus, I was startled when a young man approached me and gave me a bear hug, then began kissing me enthusiastically on both cheeks (in the Arab custom). He seemed to know me, although I could not remember having met him before, and he was extremely excited to see me. He stepped back with a big smile, and then kissed me again.

"Who is this man?" I asked the Arab brothers along with us.

"This is the pastor," they told me, "and he will explain everything to you."

As our group sat on the grass and enjoyed the refreshments served to us, the story unfolded.

This pastor began by reminding me of my first visit to the northern Galilee village in May 1987, when the lives of Beulah and I were threatened by a fanatical Moslem group.

"Yes," I said, "I remember well how the family, whose home we stayed in, was quite disturbed about the threats made to them and to the whole village if they would not order us to leave immediately."

"I was one of those men," the young leader told us, "and my assignment was to kill you or beat you if you defied the orders. In fact, I was to be given 8,000 shekels [approximately $4,000] to have you killed and half that amount if you would be only beaten.

"I have been carrying your photograph for more than a year in hopes of finding you so I could receive the reward offered to me. Different times I would ask people in the Galilee area if they knew or heard that Gerald Derstine was in the country."

By now everyone's attention was riveted on what the young Arab man was saying.

"On this certain day, the last day of April, I had come home from a fight, took a shower and laid down on my bed to rest, about one o'clock in the afternoon."

He turned toward me. "While I was lying there, you came into my room, frightening me because I did not know you were in the country. You sat next to me on my bed. I recognized you because I had your picture, and my assignment was to beat you up or even kill you if you didn't leave our villages. You had a very peaceful look on your face.

"You began to tell me about Jesus, and you answered my questions that were deep in my heart. But I knew that I had done so many terrible things in my lifetime, hurting people, that I did not think I could be forgiven.

"You assured me that I could be forgiven of all my sins. I asked you if you would pray to God and ask God to forgive me. You said, 'Yes, God forgives you.' Then you laid your hands on my head and prayed for me.

"When you were praying, a warm feeling came over me, and I felt as if a scrub brush came into my head and began scrubbing and washing my brain. Then it went down into all the rest of my body, making me clean. I became totally enlightened, a new person, all clean, and born again."

I was astonished at this story. When I checked my appointment book, I noted that I had been at a meeting in Melfort,

Saskatchewan, Canada, on April 30th. In fact, I was sleeping in someone's home, in their prophet's chamber, at the very moment this man said that I was in his room.

"In what language was I speaking to you?" I asked.

"Arabic, with our Cana dialect," he replied. "You spoke very clear and kind to me."

"I don't speak Arabic," I said. "You must have had a dream. You fell asleep on your bed and dreamed all this."

"No," he said. "I did not dream. I was not even sleeping. I had laid down, but I was awake."

Then it must have been a vision, I told him. "I was in Canada, not in Israel, on that day."

"No, you were here," he insisted.

"Please show me your room," I said then. "I would like to see where this happened." I remembered reading in the Bible about Philip and the eunuch, when God whisked Philip away in the spirit. Could God have supernaturally transported me by the spirit? I wondered.

The man took me and some of the members of our tour group into the house and into his room. He positioned himself on the bed just as he was on April 30, 1989, when this miracle took place.

"And where was I?" I asked him. The room did not look familiar to me.

He pointed to a place on the bed, about knee-high, so I walked over and sat down there. As I sat on the bed, he was suddenly overcome with the memory of what had happened.

"Oh, my God!" he exclaimed, and covered his face with his hands, reliving the visitation once again. Hugging me, he again kissed my cheeks and forehead, tears welling in his eyes.

By then we all were crying with joy and thanksgiving to God as we witnessed this unusual drama. This, I concluded, must have been an angelic visitation, a sign and wonder of the end-time.

This young man already had led about ten other men to the Lord, and was teaching the Bible to a body of believers in his home. He now has brought his family and many of the Cana villagers to a saving knowledge of Jesus Christ.

His brother, who had made all the arrangements to be trained in Cairo to become a Moslem priest, instead graduated from our ten-week Institute of Ministry in Bradenton, Florida, in April 1990.

These men must carry on their ministry underground. If they are discovered, they can be killed or their homes burned down.

Since 1981, when I had become enlightened about Israel, our congregation at Christian Retreat has been giving a monthly offering for Jacob (Israel). As a guideline for our giving, God reminded me that the children of Israel had been required to bring their first fruits, one-tenth of their income, to the priesthood. The Levites, or priests, then were to give one-tenth of this tenth to the high priests.

So I had encouraged our people to give a tithe of their tithe, equivalent to one percent of their income, to Jacob (Israel).

I believe that because of our consistent almsgiving and prayer for Israel, God saw fit to stay the killer's hand from my life. Instead, God commissioned an angel from Heaven to visit this Arab Moslem and bring him into the Kingdom of God.

Why would He have chosen that vision to happen at one o'clock in the afternoon? It just happens that at that very moment, our intercessors at Christian Retreat were praying, as they do every morning at seven o'clock.

Just as it was with Cornelius of the Bible, who through his almsgiving and prayers God blessed, so too did God bless us by converting an enemy into the pastor of our first church in Cana.

Chapter Nine

A Midnight Visitation

There were always so many children.

I learned it was not unusual for an Arab Moslem family to have 12 or more children, and with generations of families living closely together in communities, children were in abundance.

As I observed them playing in one of the villages in Galilee where we had a number of believers, I asked our leaders, "What are you doing to train the younger generation?"

"We have no one to teach them," was their reply.

"But we must teach the boys and girls," I said. "Perhaps I can send someone from America."

"No, Brother Gerald, they would not be accepted here," they said. "It must be someone from our village."

That night, the brothers prayed earnestly for God to reveal who should teach the children in that community.

God heard their cries and chose another divine visitation.

This time it happened to Katam, a talented 30-year-old Moslem mother, who was also a schoolteacher with a completely equipped preschool owned by herself and her husband...and financed by Islam.

At one a.m. on Sunday, March 11, 1990, my wife Beulah, by divine revelation, appeared to Katam and touched her on the left shoulder as she lay sleeping alongside her husband, a devout Moslem.

Katam says her bedroom seemed to radiate with a bright light as she arose from her bed, and Beulah led her by the hand down the stairs into the living room.

In the Arabic language, Beulah expounded the Scriptures, explaining to Katam a more perfect way to teach boys and girls about the way, the truth, and the life: Jesus.

At this point Katam had no idea who Beulah was. She had never met her, and yet Beulah taught her for 45 minutes, admonishing Katam to change her teachings to those of the Bible.

After Beulah departed, Katam returned to her bedroom, trembling, woke her husband and attempted to explain her encounter. Hussein, who teaches religion in a nearby public school and who had strongly resisted the new Christian believers' movement, was frightened and immediately thought his wife might be sick. "I must take you to the hospital," he said.

"No, take me to your mother," Katam told him. In their culture, if there is a conflict, the parents are consulted. Hussein's parents lived next door, perhaps 50 yards away, so they went over and awakened them.

As Katam was explaining to her mother-in-law about the strange visitation, she suddenly spotted a photo on the coffee table.

"Who is that woman?" she exclaimed.

It was a snapshot of Beulah, myself and Khalid, a 1989 graduate of our Institute of Ministry in Florida.

"That is Beulah, who lives in America where Khalid attended school," her mother-in-law replied.

At this Katam fell prostrate on her face, speechless for ten minutes. When she revived, her mother-in-law attempted to explain that Beulah was not there, but Gerald, the husband, was in the village.

"No," Katam insisted, "this lady was in my room! She, in this photograph!"

The mother-in-law then suggested that Katam relate her incredible story to our leaders, Tabari and Sa'id, who were sleeping in a home next door to Hussein's parents.

So around five a.m., the young woman awakened the two men and there, amidst praises to God, Katam gave her heart to Jesus.

That same night I had been staying in the same village in the home of one of the other believers. After breakfast we visited with Tabari and Sa'id and they excitedly related the story to me.

We walked to the home of Katam and, still trembling, she told us what she had experienced. Then she escorted us to her school room. "All this now belongs to Jesus," she said, a brilliant smile on her face. "I discarded all the Koran books and materials. I scrubbed all the floors and walls to cleanse my whole place from the false Islamic spirit."

Katam now became concerned about her husband, Hussein, who had gone to work very troubled over her condition. I suggested that we could perhaps speak to him.

The brothers and I drove to the school in the neighboring village where Hussein taught. He was expecting us, and in a private room we shared the plan of salvation with him.

God miraculously touched his heart, and he accepted Jesus as his personal Savior. With gratitude, he hugged me and kissed my cheeks. What a thrill to see God change a hard-line Islamic educator into a follower of Jesus Christ!

In my excitement, I naturally wanted Beulah to hear this story. So I telephoned her in Florida and suggested that she join me in Israel by coming with our tour, which was to depart the next day. Over the telephone, Katam also urged her to come.

Beulah did come, and what a glorious meeting! With tears in her eyes, Katam hugged and kissed Beulah, saying, "Same face, same voice!"

Later, as they sat on the sofa and talked, Katam grasped Beulah's hand and held it tightly. "I feel so right now," she said, her face beaming.

Katam's school now teaches the children about Jesus. We obtained some new Christian teaching materials for her, and the Lord even gave her a new song to teach the children.

Hussein has become a strong believer, speaking forth the Word of God boldly. With his witness and that of the other believers in the village, I would not be surprised to see that whole village turn from Islam to Jesus Christ.

There is something happening in our world, and it's happening where it all began.

We are living in the beginning of the end-time. The land where God began His work is now back in the hands of those whom He chose to be His people. When Jesus returns, He is coming back to that land—to Jerusalem.

If He's coming back to Jerusalem, He will return to a people who are anxious to see Him. Presently, the majority who live in Israel are not looking forward to His return.

But that will change.

Chapter Ten

His Land—
Our Fatherland

Why do I focus so much of my personal ministry on the land of Israel? I have a vision burning in me. In my vision, I see the Church as an army. In the past we thought that warfare was limited to casting demons out of people. But why limit the effect of this army? Our heavenly Father may have another set of orders. I believe that He really does want to restore the land that He calls "My land" in order that the world will see Jerusalem as a praise in the earth, just as He promised in His Word.

For Zion's sake will I not hold My peace, and for Jerusalem's sake I will not rest, until the righteousness thereof go forth as brightness, and the salvation thereof as a lamp that burneth.

And the Gentiles shall see thy righteousness [He has reference to the land of Israel], *and all kings thy glory: and thou shalt be called by a new name, which the mouth of the Lord shall name.*

Thou shalt also be a crown of glory in the hand of the Lord, and a royal diadem in the hand of thy God. [The prophet is talking about Jerusalem.]

Thou shalt no more be termed Forsaken [for almost 2,000 years it was a forsaken city and no nation or people had an interest in it]; *neither shall thy land any more be termed Desolate* [but it was desolate]: *but thou shalt be called Hephzibah, and thy land Beulah: for the Lord delighteth in thee* [here the prophet is again talking about the land], *and thy land shall be married.*

Isaiah 62:1-4

The Lord delights in that land. Some people may find that hard to understand. Suppose you own a piece of real estate that you prize and brings you joy—a special seaside home or cabin in the mountains. Well, God has a piece of real estate on this earth that He calls, "My land" (Jer. 2:7; Jer. 16:18; Ezek. 38:16; Joel 2:18).

Even though the whole earth is God's possession and creation, this one piece of land, the land of Israel, is special above all others. He is careful to define its borders and describes it as "the glory of all lands" (Ezek. 20:6).

Did you ever wonder why one cannot find an exact location on the earth for the Garden of Eden? Surely you would know it to be a great tourist attraction with hotels and resorts. However, perhaps because the enemy of God, satan, deceived our first parents, Adam and Eve, and started sin and death on that land, God saw to it that the exact location would never be known to the human race.

But He chose a special spot on the earth, calling it "My land," to bring the restoration and redemption of the human race through His Son, Yeshua, Jesus, born through a virgin. Then He recorded in His Word clearly defined borders for His land.

God's covenant involved not only Abraham and his seed, but also the land God chose to establish redemption for the human race. To seal that covenant, He purposed His blood to flow from the side of His Son and fall in Jerusalem, onto the land of Israel. His blood is still crying out for the souls of the earth, of all nationalities and races. God cut a covenant with that land.

Should we have an interest in this land?

We should be careful about what we say about God's land and God's people. In reality, as seed of Abraham (Christians) that land is indeed our true fatherland. Our salvation comes as a result of the happening in that land. The United States of America is a land of liberty and freedom for millions of people because of what happened in Israel.

Being of German descent, my parents taught me that Germany was my fatherland. Naturally I would get excited about someday visiting my fatherland. Later, however, I realized that being German-born was not a big deal. I was born in sin. I learned that if I remained in my sins, I would go to hell. Yes, Germany is my fatherland to my natural self, a self that needed to become quickened and totally changed. Then I heard the gospel message and became born again.

Having become born again, eternal life is now my portion and Heaven my destiny. How did that come about? It came through a man named Jesus, a Jew who was born in

Bethlehem, Israel; who was reared in Nazareth, Israel; who was crucified on a cross and shed His blood in Jerusalem, Israel; who rose from the dead and ascended to Heaven from Jerusalem, Israel; and who, the Scriptures say, is coming back to Jerusalem, Israel, again.

Being exceedingly grateful for my eternal salvation that originated in Israel, giving me a second birth, causes me to joyfully declare that surely Israel is my *true* fatherland. *Every born-again believer should recognize and declare the nation Israel as his fatherland.*

Isaiah 62:4-5 tells us more about this land that is named Beulah: "...for the Lord delighteth in thee, and thy land shall be married. For as a young man marrieth a virgin, so shall thy sons marry thee [the land]: and as a bridegroom rejoiceth over the bride, so shall thy God rejoice over thee [the land]." It is to this land that our Lord will return. He shall rule the world from this location as King of Kings and Lord of Lords. Could it be that God's army, the Church, is to play a major role in preparing the people of this land for the coming of the King, the Messiah?

Peacemaking

Psalm 122:6 says:

Pray for the peace of Jerusalem: they shall prosper that love thee.

Why will people prosper when they set their eyes on Jerusalem in this day? God is preparing the land. In our generation we are seeing literally thousands of Arabs, Muslims, Jews and Samaritans coming to their Messiah. The increase of believers will continue. It will continue to expand because God is preparing Jerusalem and the land according to His plan.

Read what He says in verses 6 and 7 of Isaiah 62: "I have set watchmen upon thy walls, O Jerusalem, which shall never hold their peace day nor night: ye that make mention of the Lord, keep not silence, and give Him no rest, till He establish, and *till He make Jerusalem a praise in the earth.*"

Present Jerusalem is not a praise on the earth. Much conflict is still there and it can't become a praise until we redeem that city from the giants. The giants are the unbelief, the haughtiness and the stiffness of some of the orthodox in both the Jewish and Islamic communities, who still resist the love that is being manifested through God's army (the Church). New Age humanistic philosophy still runs rampant in secular-minded Israel.

Actually, the majority of the Jewish population embraces liberal idealogy in lieu of the Holy Scriptures. Perhaps it will be a great war that will crack this hardness. But as the pressure becomes greater and as more of us journey to that land expressing peace and joy, truly the inhabitants will catch a glimpse of their Messiah and hope will rise.

Are we capable of going to that land called Beulah, as watchmen on the wall, confronting the people with love and forgiveness?

The apostle Paul says in Romans 11:25-26: "...blindness in part is happened to Israel, until the fulness of the Gentiles be come in. And so all Israel shall be saved: as it is written, There shall come out of Sion [Zion] the Deliverer, and shall turn away ungodliness from Jacob."

Who is her Deliverer? Yeshua, the Messiah, the one we call Jesus. We know He resides in our hearts, guiding us and anointing us to do His works, fulfilling His Father's will. Thus the Christ of Zion will deliver Zion, the nation Israel.

Our role as the Church, the Body of Christ, is to aggressively do everything in our power to love the Jew and to love the Arab who, with us, are the seed of Abraham. All three of us are children of the same Father. We're in the same family. We must concentrate our prayers on them, forgiving them as God has, favoring them, blessing them in any way we possibly can. Psalm 102:13-14 says:

"Thou shalt arise, and have mercy upon Zion: for the time to favour her, yea, the set time, is come. For thy servants take pleasure in her stones, and favour the dust thereof."

As a member of the family, I have pledged to bless my Arab and Jewish brothers with the love of our Messiah, Jesus, the only true hope for peace in our fatherland.

Chapter Eleven

A Samaritan Miracle

In my many tours to Israel, I had always been intrigued by stories of the Samaritans, a tiny tribe of ancient people who still inhabit the mountains of Samaria.

The area is rich in biblical history. God appeared to Abram there, in Shechem, promising the land to his descendents (Gen. 12:7). After crossing the Jordan and conquering the land, Joshua built an altar to the Lord on Mount Ebal, and in the presence of the Israelites wrote on the stones a copy of the law of Moses (Josh. 8:30-32).

For several generations Samaria was the capital of Israel and the dwelling of her kings and nobles. Jacob's Well, the tombs of Elisha and Obadiah, and ruins of the palaces of King Ahab and Omri can be found there.

The tightly-knit tribe of Samaritans still living in Shechem (now known as Nablus) numbers around 877 and is dwindling. I was told that they keep to themselves, resisting outside interference and marrying only within the tribe.

Historically considered Gentiles, their religion is a mixture of Jewish, Moslem and Christian. They follow the laws of the Torah, although there are slight variations between their version of the Torah and that of the Jews.

The Samaritans annually celebrate Passover on the summit of Mount Gerizim, which they consider sacred. Following the laws of the Torah, they have continued to offer animal sacrifices to atone for their sins.

Sa'id told me that he had just spent a week in the home of his friend, the high priest of the Samaritan people, and had explained the Scriptures to him.

"We discussed many things, and he now has accepted Jesus Christ and become born again," Sa'id said.

In March 1989, our Christian brothers brought this man to my hotel room in Jerusalem. We listened spellbound as he related a most remarkable story that happened late one night in January of that year—surely a modern-day sign and wonder!

A Samaritan woman from his village, he said, was expecting to give birth, but was having some difficulties with the delivery of her baby. Her friends urged her to go to the hospital, but when the priest was notified, he said, "No, first let me lay hands on her and pray in the name of Jesus, and ask God to heal her. Jesus can heal her."

Placing his hands on her head, he began to pray.

Suddenly, all those present were startled to hear a voice. At first the people thought the sound was coming from outside the house, but they soon realized it was the voice of the baby coming from inside the mother!

The cry became louder, and distinct words could be heard—words of praise to God in their ancient Samaritan language.

They were bewildered, startled and amazed when suddenly the child birthed, coming forth literally shouting the praises of God, its tiny arms waving and its eyes wide open. The infant, a boy, was alert and lively, appearing as large as a two- or three-month-old child, according to the priest.

The women in the room fell on their faces in awe. They told the priest that when they looked at him, the priest, his body was glowing with light—so much so that the whole room seemed to be brilliantly lit.

"Why do you think this happened?" I asked the Samaritan high priest.

He answered in a terse and distinct manner. "This had to happen because I was having trouble with the other priests when I was attempting to make some changes. They were scheming to replace me as the high priest because I spoke much about Jesus and wanted us to stop making animal sacrifices for our sins."

He continued, "This miracle caused them to believe that what I was telling them was right. Our people are now going to believe in the blood sacrifice of Jesus on the cross for the remission of their sins. I believe someday soon, all my people will be born again."

The priest told me that only a remnant of his people remain. They have retained their identity by forbidding their people to marry outside of their tribe; however, this has caused much physical weakness and many early deaths. He now has given Bibles to his people, and believes that they all will become believers in the Messiah. They also have relaxed the rules on intermarriage.

The following year, the priest came to visit me in Jerusalem again and brought with him David, the miracle child, along with the child's older sister.

Observing the cherubic 15-month-old boy, I asked the priest, "Is this child's life different in any way?"

"Yes," he replied, "he is a very good child. He is peaceful and kind, and does not get angry. He is quite advanced for his age."

Later the child sat quietly on my lap, showing no fear, and listened to the adults' conversation as if he understood every word.

According to our most current report from Sa'id and Tabari, 200 of the Samaritan people are now born again and have ceased offering animal sacrifices.

"Since that week, the first week of January 1989," the high priest told us, "we have agreed not to kill any more sheep and goats for their blood, and trust instead in the blood of Yeshua, Jesus Christ."

I believe that the timing of this astounding miracle is significant.

Israel celebrated its fortieth year of statehood on May 14, 1988. The entire world has experienced dramatic changes since 1988—and the miracle in Samaria, which began in 1988, was the first of many to follow. The encounter in Cana as recorded in Chapter Eight was the second dramatic miracle that year.

Chapter Twelve

The Zion of God

I was sitting in my office one day in 1987 when I received a phone call from the Secretary of the Prime Minister of Israel. At first I was startled to hear from such a high-ranking official, but I became excited as I listened to his request. He wanted to know if I would serve as a peace mediator between Jews and Arabs in the land of Israel.

"Would you come to our office on your next visit in our country?" he asked. "We want to talk to you further about this matter."

Visiting with him in Israel soon after that, I asked why they had considered me as a peace mediator. "I'm a man of God," I said, "not a politician."

The secretary to Mr. Shamir responded, "Gerald, we're not really looking for another political man. We've had the United Nations for nearly 40 years and what have they accomplished? We're still at zero with our problem.

"We've had the political system of your nation America over us for nearly 40 years and we are still at zero with our problem. Many of us in our party [Likud] talked this over and we believe if we are ever going to get off dead center with the problem between Jews and Arabs in this land, we must call upon the Christians to help us."

I was astounded to hear these words from a top government official of Israel. If it had been any other nation, I would have shown little interest. However, of all the nations on earth, this one, Israel, is known as the Holy Land, and aren't we Christians known as a holy people? God's Word is clear: "Blessed are the peacemakers: for they shall be called the children of God" (Matt. 5:9).

What if we are being called upon by God to bring a peace solution to Israel? Certainly it would seem practical for God to use holy people to resolve the problem in the Holy Land!

Romans 11:25 says that "blindness in part is happened to Israel, until the fulness of the Gentile be come in." Speaking as a prophet, Jesus Christ said in Luke 21:24 that "Jerusalem shall be trodden down of the Gentiles [meaning non-Jews], until the times of the Gentiles be fulfilled."

We are now in the 1990's. Since 1967 we have had the right to believe that the time of the Gentiles is being fulfilled. You see, everything that God does usually takes a generation or a certain span of time.

The day of grace didn't happen overnight. It began in God's mind when He decided to place the seed in the virgin Mary. She had to wait nine months for the Christ-child to be born. The world had to wait another 33½ years before the sacrificial blood was shed for all nations and

peoples through His crucifixion on the cross. It took nearly 35 years, but in God's mind He saw the day of grace at
the time the seed was put into the body of the virgin girl,
Mary—a generation.

Don't you think that the Church should have enough
of the mind of God to discern the beginning of the end of
the era known as the "times of the Gentiles" being fulfilled? I believe we are living in the later years of that time
span known as a generation. Biblically, a generation usually is 33 to 40 years, and can be even as much as 70 years.

I believe God looks upon the Church as a peacemaker
army. Surely we are not an impotent army merely to be
raptured out of this world, but rather a people equipped
with the Holy Spirit and empowered by God to administer
peace—for Christ is the answer!

He has an army for a purpose. We have His presence
and His Spirit, and He is calling us to fulfill part of His
plan for this end-time. Again, Romans 11:25-26 says that
"blindness in part is happened to Israel [referring to the
natural nation of Israel], until the fulness of the Gentile be
come in." Then the very next words are, "And so all Israel
shall be saved." It continues, "There shall come out of
Sion [Zion] the Deliverer, and shall turn away ungodliness
from Jacob."

Who or what is Zion? We know who the Deliverer is.
The Deliverer is Jesus, the Messiah. Christians claim that
He dwells inside them, here in this world. Christ is alive in
them. If He is alive in us, is He still the Son of God while
He's inside us? If He is Son of God, is He still interested
in fulfilling His Father's will? The answer to both is yes,

and if He is inside us, He can influence our mind to fulfill the Father's will.

But what caused Jerusalem to be called the City of Zion? Why does the Word of God refer to the residence of King David as Mount Zion? The whole nation became known as Zion because of God's presence in the land. Zion infers the presence of God. God met regularly with instructions for King David where the king lived on the mountain top, thus becoming known as Mount Zion. The children of Israel worshiped on the Temple Mount, meeting with God in the temple, and with the high priests, on a regular basis. Thus we have the city of Zion and the nation Zion.

The Temple of God

Does God still meet with people on the earth today? Does He have a temple on the earth today? Of course! You are the temple of God. I believe that God dwells in the Church and that Christ is alive in us. (Read First Corinthians 3:16-17.)

We are the Zion of God that contains the Deliverer of Jacob, the Deliverer who can save the nation of Israel from darkness and ungodliness. We contain the life, the enlightenment that Christ gives us, to open the blindness of Jewish Israel. (In fact, I believe every born-again believer in Messiah, Jesus, should consider himself a Zionist in the context of the Word of God because God's presence truly dwells in us—actually, more in us than on Mount Moriah or Mount Zion today.)

Deliverance will come, I believe, in the same way Jesus came to fulfill it in the first place. He came to bless His people. He knew it was His Father's will that they receive His grace and His blessing.

Look at it this way. In the beginning, the Gentiles did not have the privileges of salvation. They were lost and were not a people. Then God saw fit to open their eyes and He used Jews to show them that they were lost. He accomplished that nearly 2,000 years ago through Jesus and His Jewish disciples.

Perhaps God wants to use the Body of Christ, the Church, including the Gentiles, that He has anointed as an army, to help the rest of the world find peace on our earth. This peace will originate from Jerusalem and affect all nations of the world (Ps. 122:6).

Forty Years

Since 1988, Israel's fortieth anniversary, many significant things began happening in our world: Tieneman Square in China, the crumbling of the Berlin Wall, and the eastern bloc nations abandoning Communism and moving toward a free democracy.

Biblically, the number 40 appears to stand for God's extent of tests and trials. After 40 days or 40 years, it seems that God always does something big and new. For 40 years the children of Israel wandered in the wilderness. They came into the Promised Land after 40 years.

Forty days and nights Moses talked with God on Mount Sinai as Moses received the Ten Commandments. Jesus spent 40 days and nights in the wilderness before He entered into Galilee declaring, "the kingdom of God is at hand" (Mark 1:14-15). How exciting to think that God chooses to make the land ready for Jesus' return, and that we, the Church, should have a part in it!

I honestly believe that we as the Church have the answer for the world. But we must start now to identify with the land.

The Word of God says in Psalm 122:6, "Pray for the peace of Jerusalem: they shall prosper that love thee." Identify with that land. Many Christians are doing so by placing a menorah in a prominent place in their home.

Menorah

I believe God is raising up an army of believers who will be as flames of fire demonstrating a love, a mercy and a peace that, in turn, will overwhelm and overtake the powers of darkness in that region of the world. Churches are now being established throughout Israel, from Beersheba to Mount Hermon, the borders of Israel and Syria. The work that God has called me to do is affecting not only the Arab, but also the Samaritans and Jews.

It is because of my consistent love for the Jews that God has opened my eyes to how the Arab fits into His plan. I'll never forget a minister who chided me and said, "Gerald, why do Christian leaders only go to Israel to bless the Jews?" My answer was, "Scripture says, 'To the Jew first, and also to the Greek' " (Rom. 1:16).

"But don't you know that the problem in the land is between Jews and Arabs?" he questioned.

"If you are ever going to resolve the problem, you must minister to the Arab element as well as to the Jewish."

It is time for us to become alert and open to what God is doing.

But in the last days it shall come to pass, that the mountain of the house of the Lord shall be established in the top of the mountains, and it shall be exalted above the hills; and people shall flow unto it.

And many nations shall come, and say, Come, and let us go up to the mountain of the Lord, and to the house of the God of Jacob; and He will teach us of His ways, and we will walk in His paths: for the law shall go forth of Zion, and the word of the Lord from Jerusalem.

And He shall judge among many people, and rebuke strong nations afar off; and they shall beat their swords into plowshares, and their spears into pruninghooks: nation shall not lift up a sword against nation, neither shall they learn war any more.

Micah 4:1-3

Chapter Thirteen

"I Was Sent to Kill You"

Settling back into the sofa in Sa'id's living room, I smiled and took a deep breath.

"You know, Sa'id, I feel so peaceful here," I remarked. The sun was shining and the early fall air was dry and still reminiscent of summer. Luscious clusters of grapes hung from the arbors in nearly everyone's homes.

The young leader smiled back at me. "Praise God, Brother Gerald, I am happy that you are visiting in my house," he replied.

Several hours earlier, on my way into the Hebron area, I had watched some former Moslem sheiks sacrifice a goat that would be served later that day at a feast in my honor. This was a custom reserved for high-ranking officials, I was told. I would have been just as happy with a simple chicken dish or vegetable plate.

Accompanying me on this particular visit was my nephew, Larry Derstine, and he and I had watched the gory ritual of slashing the goat's throat to drain the blood—not a pretty sight or sound! Adding even more to the sense of adventure was the roundabout route at which we had arrived. For safety's sake, we had had to change cars three times between Jerusalem, Bethlehem and this risky territory on the West Bank.

Now, sitting in Sa'id's house, situated next to our newly-constructed "First Church of the Martyrs" that presently houses the widows and children of the martyred new believers, I felt safe.

My peace was suddenly shattered by a commotion just outside the living room door.

Before I knew what was happening, I was being motioned into the adjoining room where a masked man lay on his back on the floor. A checkered scarf was wrapped tightly around his face, with only his eyes showing. His body, seemingly unconscious, was trembling.

We immediately began praying for him, and within moments he opened his eyes, stared straight at me and leaped to his feet. To my astonishment, he threw his arms around me and began hugging me tightly.

Then, kissing my cheeks, he said in Arabic, "You are a good man, you are a good man. The old man in the mosque brainwashed my mind, telling me you are evil, an infidel, and must be killed."

As Sa'id translated the young man's words, I suddenly noticed the long, razor-sharp knife lying on the floor. This man had come to take my life!

Sa'id's wife, visibly upset, said that the man had slipped through the back kitchen door and she had been unable to stop him as he ran toward the living room.

I looked at the man again. Smooth-faced and lean as a twig, he appeared to be more boy than man. We later learned that he was just 16 years old.

"I was sent to kill you," he explained, "but when I looked at you, a bright light shone from your face." The brilliant light, he said, knocked him off his feet backward onto the floor. As he laid there, God opened his eyes to a vision of hell while a strong voice spoke, saying that the flames of fire would have devoured him if he had placed the knife in the heart of the holy man. This strong presence of God spoke to his heart to serve Messiah, Jesus Christ!

Like Saul of Tarsus on the road to Damascus, this young man's life was completely transformed from that instant. He has given his life to God and chosen to remain with our family of believers, never to darken the doorway of a mosque again.

Later that afternoon we savored the feast of goat meat prepared for us and rejoiced in the divine protection God had provided. Then for the first time I noticed that our hosts, the former Moslem sheiks, offered a prayer of thanks to God for the meal before it was served.

Like a proud papa who delights in the smallest achievements of his little ones, my heart overflowed with gratitude to God. It might not happen overnight, but these baby Christians were just as much a part of the family of God as I was, and they were destined to mature.

Chapter Fourteen

Other Signs and Wonders

Mohammed of West Bank, Judea

Realizing that we couldn't possibly bring all the new believers to our Institute of Ministry in Florida, we held a three-week Bible school in East Jerusalem in the spring of 1988. Eighteen Arab Moslem men, some married and others single, eagerly accepted the invitation to join the classes and learn from the Holy Book.

Beulah and I were warned that it would be risky to attempt such an event, particularly in Arab-dominated East Jerusalem during this politically tense time. However, we felt that God had ordained this school and that He would protect us.

I taught from a specially-prepared booklet that compared Bible scripture to writings from both the Koran and Torah. Only two of the students dropped out of the school after the second day, suspecting that I was attempting to convert them from their Islamic religion to Christianity. The remaining 16 students had a total life change, considering themselves born again through their faith in the blood atonement of Jesus Christ.

One of our most outstanding students was Mohammed, whom God so radically changed that he constantly beamed with joy. Each day God would give him some unique proverb or thought that would edify the entire class—and we marveled at the wisdom flowing from this newly-converted young man.

The change in his life affected Mohammed's family also.

"My wife says I am different," he told us. "Before, I would get mad easily, but now I am happy all the time because Jesus is in my heart." God instantly delivered him from a long-time smoking habit—another testimony to his family. In fact, this so impressed his father that he too gave up smoking!

Mohammed has become one of our most faithful leaders. Employed by the school system, his job brings him into contact with many children in that region and he has established a growing children's ministry near his home.

Several years ago, he and his family wanted to serve a meal to our entire tour group. However, he was concerned that it might not be safe for our bus to enter his neighborhood because of the hostilities.

Several weeks prior to our arrival, Mohammed had a vivid dream. In this dream he saw himself and his family eating together in the huge Christian Greek Orthodox monastery situated on the road between Jerusalem and Bethlehem. Being a Moslem, he had never stopped to visit the priest or caretakers there. However, the thought persisted that he should go and tell them his dream.

Summoning all his courage one day, Mohammed was pleasantly surprised to receive a friendly welcome, and yes, he and his family could use the facility and eat in a large room made for group functions.

Not only did Mohammed's family serve our entire group a tasty meal that year, but it also has become a tradition. Every year since then he has prepared a feast for us at the same place, serving us Arab-style on the floor. Our tour members get excited about learning to eat with their fingers, then about meeting Mohammed and his lovely family and hearing their testimony of faith in Jesus Christ.

Over the years, we have become acquainted with the old Greek Orthodox priest also, and he has welcomed us to return any time.

Healing at El Manna

Tabari tells of a miracle at El Manna, our headquarters in East Jerusalem.

He had seven men helping him make improvements to the building when one of the men slipped from the chimney and fell three stories onto a concrete floor. When they reached him, several of his teeth lay scattered on the floor, blood ran from his mouth, and he appeared unconscious or dead.

"God gave me power to pray," Tabari said. "Boldly I threw myself on him and started to pray loudly in unknown tongues. Within only one minute, God healed him. He sat up, looked around and said, 'Where are my teeth?' "

Tabari's helpers were Moslem friends who had been listening to the gospel, but who had not made a commitment. One of them asked, "What language were you talking?"

Tabari explained to them this manifestation of the Holy Spirit, and each one of the seven men became a believer. Tabari's older brother, Talel, gave his life to the Messiah and today is the head pastor of this work in East Jerusalem.

Childless Woman Conceives

Tabari and Sa'id were approached by a woman from Jordan, a special friend to Sa'id's wife. She greatly desired children, but had been unable to conceive.

The men prayed for her, and Tabari prophesied that she would have twin sons. Exactly nine months later, she did have twin boys. Needless to say, this miracle resulted in this family becoming believers in Jesus.

Sa'id Kidnapped and Tortured

Sa'id endured a terrifying experience when some members of the terrorist Islamic group Hamas came to his house, and in the presence of his wife, blindfolded him and forced him to go with them. That night, before they left, he embraced his wife and smiled at her, saying within himself, "They cannot kill me unless Jesus permits it."

Sa'id maintained this attitude over the next several days when his captors took away his clothes and imprisoned him in a chilly cave. They tortured him repeatedly, burning him with cigarettes and taunting him, trying to get him to renounce his faith in Christ.

They also questioned Sa'id about whether he was collaborating with the Israeli government.

As radical Islamic fundamentalists, the Hamas group is not just against Israeli occupation, but against Israel's very existence. They believe that Palestine should remain under Moslem control forever and that their duty is to kill every Jew or advocate of Zionism who stands in their way. They are willing to die for their extreme religious causes.

The Hamas Covenant, published in 1988, states, "Israel will exist and will continue to exist until Islam will obliterate it, just as it obliterated others before it." The group opposes all peace negotiations between Israel and Arab states.

The accusation by the radical Moslems that our men might be collaborating with Israel is quite common. When these men become born again, their attitude toward Israel is totally changed as they begin to study the Scriptures and see Jewish Israel as our Bible presents it.

They are quick to say, "This is the life that we looked for; now we have found the answer." Hatred leaves their hearts and new understanding enters in. I teach them to love everyone, and when they read the Bible for themselves, they discover that the Jews were given Israel, including Judea and Samaria (West Bank) for an everlasting possession.

They acquire a fresh love for the Jewish people, who gave us our Messiah and our Scriptures. They desire to live in peace with the Jews. "They are our cousins," they say. "Abraham is the father of us all. We can live together peacefully."

Miraculously for Sa'id, some men came to rescue him just as the order to behead him came from the terrorists' leader. Sa'id had been told he had only one hour to live. Instead, the Islamic priest who orchestrated this attack was arrested and is presently in prison, charged with this and similar crimes.

Sa'id and these fearless new believers are intent upon bringing the gospel to their people. They are praying over every Arab community in Israel, making plans to visit each one. They travel into the most troubled areas of the West Bank and Gaza Strip. God gives them supernatural protection as they go.

The Face Next to the Light

"You must join me high up in the mountain village to meet Yassir," said my Christian friend Ayob, an Arab Druze. "We work together when I am on army duty in the Israeli Defense Forces."

For more than three years, Ayob had been faithfully witnessing about his new life in Christ to his friends in northern Israel.

Yassir had rejected Ayob's words, saying, "We will not change our religion in my village."

However, one night Yassir, an army captain, was startled when in his bedroom he had a dream or vision (he's not sure which) in which he saw a blinding light. Next to the light was a face, and he heard a voice saying, "This is My messenger in the land of Israel." Then the face began to speak and say, "You must follow the ways of Ayob."

This encounter so disturbed him that the following morning Yassir journeyed in his automobile to find his Christian army buddy and tell him about the peculiar dream.

"This is God speaking to you," Ayob said excitedly. Yassir listened as his friend witnessed to him about Messiah, Jesus Christ. Then, bowing his head and heart, he became gloriously saved. A few days later Ayob baptized him in the river Jordan.

Six months later when I visited Israel, Ayob urged me to visit Yassir. By that time Yassir had led eight other men in his village to Christ.

Winding our way high into the Galilee mountains near the Lebanon border, we arrived at Yassir's house. After being led to his lovely living room and admiring his wall hangings and furniture, we began to talk. Suddenly, staring at me, Yassir exclaimed, "I met you before! I know you...where did we meet before?"

"Perhaps at one of the holy sites on one of our many tours," I replied. "You may have been on army duty guarding, and you saw me with my tour members."

"*No, no, the face!*" Placing his hands in the air and shaping a face, Yassir said excitedly, "*You are the face I saw which the light spoke about!*"

"Tell me again, Yassir, what did the light say about the face?" I asked.

Smiling broadly, he exclaimed, "The light spoke, '*This is My messenger in the land of Israel*' ...then you [the face] said to me '*You must follow the ways of Ayob.*' "

Once again I was reminded of my apostolic call to the land of the Bible, the land which God calls "My land" (Jer. 2:7; Joel 3:2). Amazingly, this incident occurred in the same region that it happened to Saul of Tarsus, on the road to Damascus.

Yassir became the leader of our first church in that village. He and his wife named their new baby daughter "Beulah," after my wife.

Miracle Reported in Newspaper

A Moslem town council leader, given up to die because of cancer, was prayed for by two of our former Moslem, now born-again, believers. Although the healing was not instantaneous, our Lord Jesus later saw fit to visit this man and heal him.

This phenomenal miracle was printed by the Moslems on the front page of one of their own newspapers. The headline read, "I Met Jesus When I Was Asleep!"

The newspaper article, later sent to me, was a great blessing and encouragement to our Arab believers in the Galilee region. Since it was published, our leader Ayob received numerous phone calls from Arab families to come and pray for their sick.

He reported that a nine-year-old boy who was sick and unable to walk for three months received a supernatural healing when Ayob prayed in the home of the family.

Angels Lock Car Doors

In the spring of 1992, my son Phil accompanied me on a mission trip to a hostile region on the West Bank in Israel. When we returned home, we learned through Sa'id that while we were visiting the Church of the Martyrs near Hebron, two Islamic officials had come with intentions to arrest me. Their strategy had been to incarcerate me overnight and in the morning bring me before an Islamic court and have me executed.

However, when they attempted to get out of their car, their doors locked and they were unable to open them! The older Islamic official, while attempting to open the door, was stricken with a stroke. One hand suddenly became paralyzed and he went totally blind. Obviously God had sent His angels to lock our enemies in their own car.

The driver and officials, determined to capture me, began following my car with their headlights off. However, at the first road crossing, a supernatural wonder happened as a huge black storm cloud swooped out of the skies to hover between our automobiles. Unable to see which direction my car turned, they became lost and confused.

According to their own words, the driver attempted to locate our car and in doing so, turned onto a lonely road and drove off the side into a ravine, crashing the car. Still locked inside, unable to escape, they remained there for three days and nights.

Their incredible story is that on the third day they saw me, Gerald Derstine, walk up to the car. As I opened the car door, the blind man received sight in one eye and they eagerly listened to me explain Jesus to them.

The driver and two officials walked to Sa'id's house, requesting prayer, and today they are born-again believers in Jesus Christ.

When I visited that area in October 1992, the officials held a special feast honoring me in this West Bank Islamic village. Five other sheiks attended this historic meeting and they all repented in my presence. Today, one of these officials conducts Bible teachings in his home twice weekly.

My appearance to these men locked in their car was supernatural; it had to be angelic, another sign and wonder.

Sheik Healed Through Late Night Visitation

A 75-year-old Islamic sheik who had ordered an attack against our Christian believers, causing three deaths, six hospitalizations and four burned-down houses, was stricken with a severe heart condition. He was a high-ranking official whose approval and signature was required on the marriage documents of all who lived in that area.

Sa'id and his wife went to pray for this man who was close to death, but they saw no visible changes.

Early the next morning, however, the man knocked on Sa'id's door, asking to talk with Gerald and Beulah Derstine. He claimed that during the night, Gerald and Beulah Derstine visited him, saying, "I am on a quick trip...can't stay long..." and laid hands on him. The man was totally and instantly healed!

He relinquished all his religious and political ties with Islam and joined the believers.

This incident happened in August 1992. In October I met this man personally and today we have a very close relationship. My only explanation is that again God chose to supernaturally use my wife and I to save this man's life and lead him into God's Kingdom—another sign and wonder.

* * * * *

I believe in the supernatural. I believe in miracles.

In my book *Following the Fire*, I tell how early in our ministry in 1955, Beulah and I lived through a phenomenal visitation from God that lasted seven days and nights. We were conservative Mennonites then, totally unfamiliar with the supernatural power of God.

We only knew that we wanted more of God, and after a year of praying for revival, He descended upon our small mission church and home in northern Minnesota. The strange happenings that occurred were beyond our control, and it resulted in our being silenced at that time from the Mennonite Church.

But it also catapulted us into a new relationship with God that revolutionized our lives and fired us with a burning desire to preach the gospel to the ends of the earth. God has certainly brought that to pass over the past four decades.

During that revival in 1955, God spoke to us prophetically, saying, "There will be revival coming upon the face of the earth as no man has ever witnessed—even greater than what took place on the Day of Pentecost." He added that the revival to date had gone only as far as "one and one-half drops in a ten-quart pail."

I believe that what has happened over the recent ten years is further fulfillment of that 1955 prophecy. As miraculous as that experience was, the signs and wonders happening in Israel are among the most amazing we have ever witnessed. Sometimes we feel as though we are living in the Book of Acts.

I can only conclude that God is intervening in so many miraculous ways because we are approaching the end of this age. The Scriptures declare that the gospel will be preached to all the world, and then the end will come. We know that through the media of print, radio and television, the gospel indeed has been preached in the "uttermost part of the earth" (Acts 1:8).

Now, coming full circle, the gospel is being heard and believed in the land that God calls "My land." He is fulfilling His covenant with the seed of Abraham, which includes not only the descendents of Isaac and Jacob, but also the sons of Ishmael (today's Arabs) and the sons of Keturah.

The miracles that we have recounted here (and they are continuing to happen) are part of the end-time events that God is sovereignly bringing to pass to fulfill His promises. When Messiah comes, He will find believers in Israel to welcome Him: Spirit-filled Arabs, Jews and Christians, all professing to be the "seed of Abraham."

It is time to look up, for our redemption draws nigh!

Chapter Fifteen

Fulfilling the Mission

I don't know exactly why God chose me to play a central part in this Middle East revival. However, I am convinced that these miraculous happenings leave us with a mission to fulfill.

I have always felt that there is more to God's plan of redemption than simply getting saved in preparation for Heaven. The people of God who have gone before us are no different than we are. From the beginning, God's plan was to redeem the people on this earth.

First He called Abram out of Ur and showed him the way to Canaan (present-day Israel). Then He changed Abram's name to Abraham and spoke to him, saying, "From you will be the blessing of the nations. There will be kingdoms coming from you. Nations will come from you" (see Gen. 17:3-6). From these words we can see that, from the beginning, God had an intense interest in *the people* of the nations of the world. He chose the land of Israel as the nation from which the redemption and restoration of the human race should *originate and be consummated.*

Has God suddenly lost this interest? Did He lose it when He opened the door for the Gentiles to be saved? Two thousand years ago Jesus opened the door for the Gentiles and now there are millions of them who are believers in Jesus Christ. Paul, a Jewish apostle, said in short, "Those of us who have been born again, we have become a part of the commonwealth of Israel" (see Eph. 2:11-13). This indicates that we also are in the family of Israel; sons of Abraham, Isaac and Jacob. That is why Christians have an affinity toward Jews. We cannot love Christ and dislike or ignore the Jews. Christians naturally love Jews if they understand their heritage according to the Holy Scriptures.

No, God has neither changed His mind nor deviated from the completion of His plan. God still has a plan for all the nations of the world, just as He had from the beginning.

God told Abraham that his first-born son, Ishmael, would be fruitful and that God would make a great nation of him. According to Genesis 17:20, God established a covenant with him to guarantee this promise. Today there are 22 nations that come from this seed of Ishmael. There are more than 220 million Arabs who come from the seed of Ishmael, the first-born son of Abraham.

Our Roots in Abraham

Abraham is also the father of the Jewish people and the nation of Israel. *Through the Jewish people in general, and through Jesus Christ in particular, the Body of Christ is established.* Christians are found in all nations of the world. The United States has been considered a Christian nation. Canada is considered a Christian nation. The people of these and many other Christian nations have come from the seed of Isaac, Abraham's *second* son, to fulfill God's Messianic covenant with Abraham. God chose Abraham because he was a man of faith, a man He could trust to uphold his part of the covenant.

I believe that the Christian church, in this end-time, must take a new look at faith. Faith in its first steps is designed to benefit an individual alone. It is supposed to be directed toward God and utilized in fulfilling His plan and purpose on this earth, which involves nations.

God has a plan and will use people like us to fulfill His plan. As a believer in God, as a worshiper of God, as one who willingly accepted God, you and I should take an interest in the plan of God. We should want to get involved with what God is doing, even to the point of relinquishing our own plans.

I had to surrender such plans in my own life. I have gone through plateaus of growth and development in my Christian experience. In the beginning I acted only on what I was taught and my level of faith was quite small. But then as I grew older in the Lord, I began seeing more clearly. The clearer the vision became, the more I was able to do. Today my thoughts are different from what they were when I first started my Christian walk more than 40 years ago. I also feel a responsibility to explain to my generation the things I have learned.

Knowing the Signs of the Times

In this generation things are changing rapidly. I'm mindful of the words of Jesus to the blind Pharisees and Sadducees in Matthew 16:1-3:

The Pharisees also with the Sadducees came, and tempting desired Him that He would shew them a sign from heaven.

He answered and said unto them, When it is evening, ye say, It will be fair weather: for the sky is red.

And in the morning, It will be foul weather to day: for the sky is red and lowring. [Then He talks to them somewhat harshly] *O ye hypocrites, ye can discern the face of the sky; but can ye not discern the signs of the times?*

Do we discern the time in which we are living? Ever since the early days of my Christian experience, I was told that we are living in the *end-time*.

When you first accept the gift of salvation, you are fulfilled being saved. That is as it should be. You are a baby and babies don't have very much responsibility. Someone else cares for them. But you don't stay a baby forever, and if you are normal, you mature.

If you realize that you are a normal Christian, then you mature to the point where you realize that you are a responsible child of God, a son of God, a servant of God. You are a responsible individual designed to fulfill something that God your Father has planned for the nations, for the peoples of this earth.

During the days following the age of Jacob and Joseph, the children of Israel lived in Egypt for more than 400 years. It was one big Israeli family from the seed of Abraham, Isaac and Jacob: 12 tribes in all. They entered the land with 80 people and they multiplied until there were more than two million Israelites. For more than 400 years, Egypt was the only home they knew.

Compare their situation with our position in the United States. Our country is slightly over 200 years old. Most of us have been living in this land for less than 100 years. Still, we think we're pretty well established.

Preparing for Change

What if the God of Abraham, Isaac and Jacob would speak to His people in the United States, to those who claim to be led by the Holy Spirit? What if God sent a prophet to declare that He has a mission for us, a mission designed to move us from our present land to a land of His choosing, thus resulting in drastic changes?

The children of Israel had to go through drastic changes. They had to pull up stakes, pack all their belongings, cross the Red Sea and go out into the wilderness. Had they not been faithful, not one of us would ever have been saved. Let us thank God for those people who were obedient and followed Moses into the wilderness and Joshua into the Promised Land.

A popular misconception of the modern Christian is of a born-again Gentile being saved primarily to go to Heaven. In the meantime, they discover God's blessings (promises) and indulge themselves until the rapture or the coming of the Lord.

What if God would again say to His Church, His anointed ones, "I want you to understand something. You are now living in a different period of time. Once again I have something you need to know, something urgent for the sake of the nations of the world and, in fact, for the whole human race." Are we willing to be led by the Holy Spirit?

Focus on what you think God's plan and purpose is at this time for the earth and the people of the earth. What is in His heart? What do we find in the Scriptures to help us discern God's heart?

Does God still love this world? We know for sure that He did when He sent Jesus. The Bible tells us, "For God so loved the world, that He gave His only begotten Son, that whosoever believeth in Him should not perish, but have everlasting life" (John 3:16). That was spoken nearly 2,000 years ago.

Something similar was spoken even before that by the prophet Isaiah. The words are different, but the intent is the same. Isaiah 11:9 says in part, "For the earth shall be full of the knowledge of the Lord, as the waters cover the sea."

The prophet Habakkuk also prophesied something similar: "For the earth shall be filled with the knowledge of the glory of the Lord, as the waters cover the sea" (2:14). So we have both Habakkuk and Isaiah saying that God will cause the knowledge of His glory to cover the earth, to fill the earth, as waters cover the sea. Let's ponder the words in Isaiah 61:11:

> *For as the earth bringeth forth her bud, and as the garden causeth the things that are sown in it to spring forth; so the Lord God will cause righteousness and praise to spring forth before all the nations.*

As believers in God, we should assume that these words of the prophets will come to pass. You may say, "It doesn't appear as though the knowledge of the glory of God is covering America today. Look at the statistics of increased violence and all kinds of upheavals in our country." Yes, it may appear as though God made a mistake when He spoke those words through His prophets. But, in reality, His knowledge and glory is covering the earth.

In Isaiah 11, God gives us a solution. He tells us how He will bring forth this knowledge that will cover the earth as the waters cover the sea. In Isaiah 11:1-2 He says, "And there shall come forth a rod out of the stem of Jesse, and a Branch shall grow out of his roots: and the spirit of the Lord shall rest upon Him...."

These verses mean, I believe, that the rod that comes out of the stem of Jesse is Jesus. He comes as a Deliverer and as a Savior.

Furthermore, I believe the branch that will grow out of Jesus' roots is the Church. So this rod coming out of Jesse is known as the Deliverer. "And there shall come forth a rod out of the stem of Jesse."

Jesse was the father of King David, a man after God's own heart—a symbol of the coming Messiah, our Savior Jesus Christ. The branch that comes from Yeshua is the Church, which includes all who have been born into the commonwealth of Israel. It includes every Jew, Arab and Gentile who is born again with that spirit of Messiah. Together we are joined into the commonwealth of Israel, worldwide. There's only one God, one Lord and one faith.

Should we consider the thought outlandish for the Church to be called upon as peacemakers, and literally arm our thinking to redeem the *Holy Land* once again?

Redemption had its beginning in Israel through Abraham. Our Redeemer was born and lived in the land of Israel. Our Father promised, from Jerusalem, Israel, that Messiah Jesus Christ shall rule and reign over the nations. Also, His coming is relative to Jerusalem, not to any other city on this earth. There is an answer to the Middle East crisis. The answer is related to Abraham's seed. Once again God may call on His mighty warriors armed with His Word and carrying peace in their loins, faith in their hearts and great joy in their spirits. I believe the answer has come!

Chapter Sixteen

Israel: Three People Groups

You don't have to be a Jew to be considered a part of Israel. Three distinct groups of people in our world can be considered Israel.

The Nation: Israel

Of the more than five million people populating the present nation of Israel, more than 750,000 are Arabs, Israeli Arabs. Many Arab Moslems actually serve in the Israel Defense Forces (IDF).

Why would Arabs serve in the Israeli Army? They are Israeli citizens by choice. Since 1948, hundreds of thousands of Arabs have chosen to be citizens of Israel, to submit to the government and the leadership of this democratic Jewish nation. They have jobs, homes and businesses. They lead a peaceful life—living on the same land, together.

Jewish People: Israel

The second group considered to be Israel in our world are the Jewish people. Approximately 18 million Jews are scattered throughout the world. They know that they are from the seed of Abraham, Isaac and Jacob.

Although they are Jews, they are not necessarily believers in God. They may be Jewish atheists, religious Jews or nonreligious Jews, but they recognize their Jewish heritage.

They are usually referred to as "Israel" or "Judah," but the New Testament describes them as being in blindness to their Messiah. The Messiah (Jesus) came nearly 2,000 years ago to bless them, but most did not accept Him as Messiah when He walked on the earth.

Their sins were identical to those living 500 years earlier, who were taken captive by King Nebuchadnezzar of Babylon and remained captive for 70 years (II Kings 25). Those who rejected Him while He was alive on earth, and most Jews living today, still look for the Messiah to come for the first time.

Because of the Jews' blindness and through God's mercy and grace, God gave the Gentiles (non-Jews) the privilege of receiving the blessing of Abraham, Isaac and Jacob (Rom. 11:7-11). Thus, those who accepted Jesus became enlightened while the rejecting Jews remained blind. Although these Jews are still Israel, they are *blind Israel* (Rom. 11:25). Their fall was God's way of fulfilling His covenant with Abraham in Genesis 12:3b: "And in thee shall all families of the earth be blessed." Genesis 17:4b says, "And thou shalt be a father of *many* nations." This means both *Jew and Gentile* nations.

The apostle Paul confirms, in Romans 11:25, that the nation of Israel is living in darkness. The Jewish people are living in ungodliness. The conflict is between their own citizens, Jews and Arabs. The Jewish nation, as a people, are blind to God's Messianic promises.

The Church: Israel

The third group of people considered Israel today is the Church. We born-again believers are in the commonwealth of Israel through the process of adoption (Eph. 2:11-13). That is why we love the Jewish people and the land of Israel. The land and the people are a part of our heritage. Without the Israeli Jew, we would not have our Bible. We know that the books of the Bible were written by Jews; thus, the born-again Christian has an affinity toward Jews because Christians love their Bible.

We also know that, according to the New Testament, the mother of Jesus was a Jewish girl, a virgin named Mary. God also chose a Jewish man by the name of Joseph to be an earthly father to our Lord Jesus, the Messiah.

Another reason we can love Jews is that our heritage is the result of their faithfulness some 3,000 years ago. Moses led them out of Egypt and they wandered in the wilderness for 40 years until Joshua led them into the land of Canaan, the Promised Land. These children of Jacob (Israel) included one of Jacob's sons, Judah. From the tribe (family) of Judah came the forefathers of King David and his son, King Solomon, who built a temple to preserve the law of Moses through the priesthood and to provide a place of worship to God for the people.

It was from the lineage of Judah that, biblically, the lineage of the Jews originated and that Jesus subsequently came to us. He came through the faithfulness of the Jewish people. Therefore we are considered Judeo-Christian.

Today Jews still populate our world and I can express my thanks to them. As an American, I am doubly thankful. If it were not for the nation of Israel, the birthplace of Jesus Christ, there never would have been a free country like America. It is thanks to the teachings of Moses and Jesus that the U.S. exists.

It is a sad day for America today when the laws deprive the public school system of reading the Bible or conducting prayer to God on school property. A nation that forgets God is on a downward spiral. God's judgment is imminent.

Three People Groups: Seed of Abraham

Similarly, there are three distinct peoples in our world that, biblically, may be considered the seed of Abraham.

The Arab seed of Ishmael, Abraham's first son, was 13 years old before Isaac, Abraham's second son, was born. The Jew has his origin from the lineage of Isaac, Jacob and Judah.

You may hear the Jew often refer to the God of Abraham, Isaac and Jacob while the Arab often refers to the God of Abraham and Ishmael. Both have their heritage in Abraham.

Christians see their heritage through Jesus Christ, born of the virgin Mary nearly 2,000 years ago, whose lineage was from the tribe of Judah, one of Jacob's sons, who came from Abraham.

Now we see all three people groups—Arabs, Jews and Christians—claim Abraham as the father of their godly heritage. Of these three groups, who claims the possession of the Holy Spirit, the Prince of Peace, and the Messiah, as well as access to both the Old and New Covenant of God? Yes, it is the Christian who experiences a transformation of his heart toward God and who is committed to serving the one and only living God.

Also, isn't it amazing how God makes all three people groups highly visible through the scrutiny of the media? All the world knows about the Arab mentality, the Jewish mentality and the Christian mentality. To finish God's plan for the nations, internationally, these three people groups must play a major role because they are the seed of Abraham through whom God's covenant shall be fulfilled.

Yes, you may very well be involved in the Middle East conflict primarily because *you are seed of Abraham*.

Chapter Seventeen

Why Is His Land Called Holy?

Have you ever wondered why the Holy Land is called "holy"? Why has it been singled out from all the lands of the earth and given God's special blessing? God must have had a purpose and a reason for doing that.

The giving of the land, and the blessing that followed the gift, begins with the call of Abram. You may wonder why God asked Abram to leave his home in Ur in the southern part of Mesopotamia, which is present-day Iraq, and go to another land. For some reason God did not want to give Abram the reason behind His request while Abram lived in Ur.

Abram was faithful to God's call and, with his wife and a few relatives, he left his home and ended up in the land of Canaan. When he arrived in this land, Abram built an altar unto his God, our heavenly Father.

It was in this land that God changed Abram's name to Abraham and told Abraham that he would be the father of many nations. Because Abraham was obedient to God's commands, God's plan was set in motion, a plan that included the coming of Jesus Christ, the Messiah; a plan to include the redemption of the whole human race.

For a long time I thought that the only people who concerned themselves about Abraham were the Jewish people. But I have since learned that the Arab people are also very much interested in Abram and the blessings that come through him. In Genesis 12:3, God made a covenant with Abram and said that He would bless all who bless Abram and He would curse all who curse Abram. This covenant blessing has been upheld by the Arab and the Jew for thousands of years.

They knew that every person who could look to Abram as "Father" was seed of Abraham. This includes the people who are known today as Arabs, descendents of Abraham through his first son, Ishmael.

In fact, Ishmael was Abraham's only son for 13 years. He was the only son that had a part in the early covenant God made with Abraham. It was Ishmael who had his foreskin cut and shed blood with his father, Abraham, making a covenant with our heavenly Father as recorded in Genesis 17. Ishmael was there before there was even a thought of an Isaac, or of a Jewish nation.

So you can understand that God loved Ishmael because of the covenant He made with Abraham and his seed, which He has not altered or changed. I had not fully grasped the importance of this relationship for a long time, even though I knew the story from the Bible.

God gave Abraham a second son, Isaac, through whom He chose to *establish* His covenant. It was through Isaac that He would bring to pass the *Messianic blessing* that included you and I. Jesus Christ, the Messiah, is a descendent of Isaac, heir to this same covenant.

Without Jesus, none of us would be united to God the Father. We would have no interest in the words of God or in the things of His Kingdom. Abraham's obedience is the basis that God used to bring us Jesus and, because of Jesus, we have Christians.

Nevertheless, we did have Jews before Jesus, didn't we? We also had Arabs before Jesus. What is unusual is, even though Abraham actually is the father of our faith, many of us thought Jesus was the father of our faith. No, Abraham was the one who obeyed God and because of Abraham's obedience, God honored him and caused him to be a blessing to all the families of the earth.

At the right time, through the lineage of Abraham, Isaac and Jacob, God saw fit to bring a Savior and through this Messiah's blood, any human can be forgiven. Unlike the people of the Old Testament who looked to the blood of sheep, goats or birds for forgiveness, Jesus, the Messiah, brings forgiveness to all through His blood—thanks to the grace of God and our faith in Him (Eph. 2:8).

Those who accept Jesus and His blood sacrifice have been grafted into the family through the process of adoption and, according to Scriptures, are also through this process born into the family of the people known as Israel. We become a part of the commonwealth of Israel.

Ephesians 2:11-18 (NAS) tells us about the way in which we have become a part of the commonwealth of Israel. It reads:

Therefore remember, that formerly you, the Gentiles in the flesh, who are called "Uncircumcision" by the so-called "Circumcision," which is performed in the flesh by human hands—

remember that you were at that time separate from Christ, excluded from the commonwealth of Israel, and strangers to the covenants of promise, having no hope and without God in the world.

*But now in Christ Jesus you who formerly were far off **have been brought near by the blood of Christ.***

*For He Himself is our peace, **who made both groups into one, and broke down the barrier of the dividing wall,***

*by abolishing in His flesh the enmity, which is the Law of commandments contained in ordinances, that in Himself He might make the two into one new man, **thus establishing peace,***

and might reconcile them both in one body to God through the cross, by it having put to death the enmity.

And He came and preached peace to you who were far away, and peace to those who were near [Jesus, the Messiah, brought peace to the Gentiles as well as to His own, the Jewish people];

for through Him [Jesus, the Messiah] *we both have our access in one Spirit to the Father.*

After reading this, we, as born-again believers in Jesus Christ, should be fully convinced that we are a part of Israel.

But there is more. Verse 19 continues, "So then you are no longer strangers and aliens, but you are fellow citizens with the saints, and are of God's household."

If I'm a part of God's household, I am in line for the blessings that God has promised to the seed of Abraham. Since I have a stake in the promises, I also have a part in the problems in Israel today. I'm related to the same issue in the Middle East that all the nations of the world say they are trying to solve.

When God made a covenant with Abraham and his seed, then you and I, as the seed of Abraham, became a part of God's plan. I say "a part of God's plan" because in addition to the covenant God made with Abraham, which now includes the Body of Christ, He made another covenant with the land, a physical piece of real estate.

For most of us, the concept of a covenant with the land is foreign, one of which we have little or no knowledge. For years it really hasn't been important for us to be concerned about this covenant. But the events of recent years have made it very significant.

In Genesis 17:7-8 God says, "And I will establish My covenant between Me and thee and thy seed after thee in their generations for an everlasting covenant, to be a God unto thee, and to thy seed after thee. And I will give unto thee and to thy seed after thee, *the land* wherein thou art a stranger, *all the land of Canaan, for an everlasting possession*; and I will be their God."

These words were spoken almost 2,000 years before Christ was born. God spoke to Abraham and established a covenant with him concerning this particular land that would be an everlasting possession for Abraham and his seed. (Also read Psalm 105:6-11.)

Approximately 110 years later, God reaffirms this covenant with Isaac, Abraham's second son. He says to Isaac in Genesis 26:3-5:

Sojourn in this land, and I will be with thee, and will bless thee; for unto thee, and unto thy seed, I will give all these countries, and I will perform the oath which I sware unto Abraham thy father;

And I will make thy seed to multiply as the stars of heaven, and will give unto thy seed all these countries; and in thy seed shall all the nations of the earth be blessed;

Because that Abraham obeyed My voice, and kept My charge, My commandments, My statutes, and My laws.

When God said this to Isaac, he was already in the land of Canaan.

The Twins, Esau and Jacob

Genesis 35:12 states, "And the *land* which I gave Abraham and Isaac, to thee I will give it, and to thy seed after thee will I give the land." Approximately 70 years later, Jacob, Abraham's grandson, was born. He was actually a twin and his brother's name was Esau. Perhaps you do not remember that Esau married the daughter of Ishmael, but Moslem Arabs are aware of this fact. Most Christians don't know of this relationship.

When I first read about this marriage, I remember thinking, "Who cares who Esau married?" Well, we should care, because there's a problem in the land, and it happens to be with Arabs and Jews who are fighting over the land that God gave to the seed of Abraham.

Every Moslem is taught that Esau, the first-born, had the birthright instead of Jacob. We know that, according to our Scriptures, this is true. At least, for a while, he had the birthright. He was the first-born. The first-born receives the birthright, which carries with it the inheritance and the blessing of the father.

To understand how the Arab views this issue, you must first understand that the book he accepts as final authority, the Koran, tells them that Esau is the legitimate heir. Esau married Ishmael's daughter and that gives them a right to the inheritance. They are also the seed of Abraham and Isaac and, as a result, they have rights to the land.

What most Arabs of today don't know is what is recorded in the Bible. They are not aware that Jacob bought the birthright from Esau, with the help of their mother, who favored Jacob. Jacob, not Esau, received Isaac's final birthright blessing. Even though the Arab Moslem does not read our Bible, we must not think that they are obtuse. Your heavenly Father loves them, and still has a covenant on their behalf (Gen. 17:20).

Do you believe that we're getting closer to the coming of the Lord? If so, do you think that God would like to see the conflict over the land resolved? After all, He's returning to that land, to the city of Jerusalem. So we as believers in Christ must recognize our responsibility before God to help solve the problem.

Perhaps the major factor in making this land of Israel holy is the blood of God that perpetually forgives sins.

The blood of Messiah Yeshua (Jesus), from His crucifixion in Jerusalem nearly 2,000 years ago, still cries mercy, grace and forgiveness.

The blood from the soil of Jerusalem still atones for one's sins, enabling sinful humanity to become born again. Why shouldn't this land be considered holy? There was only one major sacrifice made to atone for all the sins of the world: the man Jesus Christ, Son of the most Holy God (John 3:16).

Israel's border is clearly defined in the Bible—no other country in the world has clearly defined borders recorded in the Holy Bible; only Israel, the Holy Land.

Chapter Eighteen

A Symbol to the Nations

And in that day there shall be a root of Jesse, which shall stand for an ensign of the people; to it shall the Gentiles seek: and His rest shall be glorious.

Isaiah 11:10

The words of the prophet Isaiah, "*in that day,*" refer to the time of the Messiah, the time of Jesus. We are in that day. (Remember that Isaiah wrote about 700 years before Jesus came, so it was not "in that day" when Isaiah penned these words.)

Ensign means "symbol," as in a flag symbolizing a nation. Isaiah says, in effect, "There will be a root of Jesse that will stand as an ensign of the people." Jesse was the father of David, who was a type of Jesus. The root of Jesse is literally Jesus. "He stands as an ensign for the people and the Gentiles still seek Him and discover His rest to be glorious." Those of us who have found Jesus have discovered His rest, His peace.

> *And it shall come to pass in that day, that the Lord shall set His hand again the **second time** to recover the remnant of His people, which shall be left, from Assyria, and from Egypt, and from Pathros, and from Cush, and from Elam, and from Shinar, and from Hamath, and from the islands of the sea.*
>
> *And He shall set up an **ensign for the nations**, and shall assemble the outcasts of Israel, and gather together the dispersed of Judah from the four corners of the earth.*

Isaiah 11:11-12

Note the *"second time" element* in this prophecy. The first time was when the King of Babylon, after 70 years of captivity, released the people of Judah (Jews) to return and rebuild the temple. A remnant returned who rebuilt the walls of the city and restored temple worship. However, after some 500 years, the coming of the Messiah (Jesus) was rejected and once again the children of Israel were captured and scattered by the Romans in A.D. 70. Now in our time, the twentieth century, is the second time they return again and rebuild their state.

Our generation is witnessing the fulfillment of this prophecy. In 1948, we saw the return of the land of Palestine to the Jewish people and the state of Israel inaugurated.

Jews are returning to their homeland, the land to which God initially led them. We have lived to see the day that Jerusalem, their capital city, was returned to them. Before 1967, it was a divided city. When the Jewish army took control of Jerusalem during the Six-Day War, the walls came down and it was made free for all people.

The world, however, is not comfortable with the Jews in control of Jerusalem. The United Nations favors a divided Jerusalem: part Arab under PLO control and part Jew. Our nation approves of this position also at the time of this writing.

That position is contrary to God's will, against God's Word and against His plan. Jerusalem must remain a city united under the control of the Israeli government—ultimately a theocratic government (Jer. 30:3).

There are those who want to divide it once again, allowing the Palestinian Arabs (PLO) to have their capital in a portion of the city and coerce the Jews to retain another part of the city for their capital. Unfortunately, if that scenario would develop and Jerusalem came under divided control of the Arabs and the Jews, millions of Muslims would come to visit the mosque of Omar, Islam's third most holy place in the world. That is not acceptable because Islam is not compatible with the Jewish religion or the Christian faith. Their holy book, the Koran, considers the Jew and Christian as an enemy, and thus infidels. Their fundamental belief is that all infidels must be removed to allow Islam to reign.

The ultimate goal of fundamentalist Islam is to kill the Jew and the Christian. That is a part of Islam's fundamental beliefs and as a religion it is serious about carrying out those beliefs. According to the religious Moslems' way of thinking, peace occurs when the whole world is subject to Islamic rule.

However, according to God's plan, the nation of Israel shall be an *ensign or symbol to the nations* as Jesus is an ensign, a symbol to the people who turn to Him for salvation. Any nation that blesses Israel will be blessed (Ps. 122:6.). Any nation that comes against Israel will be destroyed.

Notice how the nation of Israel continues to remain in the forefront of international concern. Israel as a nation always seems to bear the blame for the various skirmishes, according to popular opinion and the media. That may be God's way of focusing world attention upon this sacred piece of land called the Holy Land. Events originating from this land have a way of shaping the course and destiny of all nations of the world. History has proven that to be so. God's way and plan as revealed in the Holy Bible will ultimately prevail. Israel, the nation, truly is a symbol or ensign to the nations of the world.

It is not only the Islamic religion, however, that creates conflict between the nations and the Arab countries in the Middle East. Another cause is oil, a resource precious to the whole world. Politically, the nations must stay friends with the Islamic people so they can keep operating automobiles and modern appliances. Modern technology relies heavily upon oil.

As we purchase their oil, we also build up the satanic empire of Islam. Islam has little power or force without American dollars. Billions and billions of American dollars flow into Saudi Arabia, Kuwait, and other Moslem Middle East countries.

We are now living in a time when all the conditions are upon the world for a possible triggering of a battle of the nations (i.e., the war of Armageddon [Joel 3:1-2]).

Isaiah said that God will set up an ensign at the time He assembles the outcasts of Israel and gathers together the dispersed of Judah from the four corners of the earth. Pray and ask God to reveal His pure Word in your heart. Attempt to discern the signs of the times (Matt. 16:1-3).

It is difficult to get people to re-evaluate their theology and to change their thinking. I often wonder what side I would have been on if I had lived in the time of Jesus. For thousands of years the people obeyed the law of Moses. Then Jesus comes on the scene, and from Nazareth of all places. It would have been easier to accept Jesus had He begun in Jerusalem. Nazareth was a Gentile city and He was a Jew claiming to be the Messiah. It was almost impossible to believe. That difficulty commonly appears any time God moves because the mind-set of the people in any generation is hard to change. We tend to become victims of tradition and culture.

It doesn't matter how born again or how saved we say we are, if we don't keep our eyes and minds focused on what God is doing and humble ourselves before God, we'll miss it in this day too.

If you are more proud of your denomination than anything else, you'll miss it. If you are boasting about some personality you are following, you won't see the truth. Anyone who walks with God is open to all of God's people. You don't prefer one group or leader over another.

We are to follow the Word of God and keep our eyes on the Lord. I claim to be no more than a teacher and a brother in the Lord. We need each other and we need to encourage and help each other.

Chapter Nineteen

The Christian Nation and Israel

Thirteen years after the war of 1967, Israel's Prime Minister Menachem Begin declared Jerusalem as the capital city. I shouted "Hallelujah" as I watched the announcement on television. The United Nations, however, was unhappy about it. Determined to stop the Jews from making Jerusalem their capital city, they went into session and came out the next day with a plan to boycott Israel. They suggested that nations remove their embassies from Jerusalem. All 13 countries that had embassies in Jerusalem in 1980 obeyed the United Nations.

That action was very significant. The message to Israel was that not one country on this earth agreed with Prime Minister Begin's decision. Every country either knows nothing of biblical truth or they're not willing to stand by the biblical mandate. They do not believe that Israel has the right to call Jerusalem their capital. Even the United States of America, a traditional friend and supporter of Israel, sided with the secular countries.

When the nations of the world in 1980 refused to honor the decision of former Prime Minister Begin, the Jewish people were humbled. They were ready to listen to another nation, a holy nation, not a secular nation. Thus, the International Christian Embassy, Jerusalem, was born, and since then, tens of thousands of Christians from around the world have come to express their love and support for Israel.

The Church, a Holy Nation

Israel may be called the Holy Land, but there is also a holy nation that can be found in all the nations of the world. Its inhabitants are known as Christians, born-again Christians, people who are quickened by the Spirit of God. You may ask, "Are Christians really a nation?" What makes a nation? First, it is people. Second, a nation must have a king or a leader. We have a King and His name is Jesus. Third, there must be a government. Our government is the Church. Fourth, a government requires a law book or a constitution. We have that in our Bible.

The uniqueness of our nation is our location. We are located in all the nations of the world.

With which group of people on the earth would Christians feel an obligation to converse? Our heritage: Jewish Israel that is today a bona fide nation with a capital city.

In the history of Christian faith, except for the first 30 years, we were without a country. It was taken away from the early Christians by the Roman Emperor Titus, the general who came to Israel from Rome in A.D. 70. He laid siege throughout the land. The temple was demolished and the city was destroyed. Israel ceased to exist as a geographic nation, and the people were scattered throughout all the world.

For almost 2,000 years, there was no nation of Israel. But in 1948, the land was restored to the Jewish people and since 1980, they have had an officially declared capital.

Many in the secular world live in darkness instead of light, which is provided by the truth. The truth is Jesus Christ, the Messiah, who lives in and through a people known as the Church.

The International Christian Embassy, Jerusalem

It is estimated that there are 1.8 billion Christians in the world. In the United States alone there are an estimated 73 million evangelical Christians. That makes a huge army of people. Now we can help the world. We Christians have an embassy in Jerusalem Israel. We have a right to it because we're a holy people and, naturally, we want our embassy to be in the Holy Land. Why would we need a dialogue with any other nationality unless we are helping them along the path to peace and enlightenment?

Now we have an obligation to the land, to make the land ready for the coming of our King. Every year since 1980, Christians from all over the world have been coming to Jerusalem, fulfilling Zechariah 14:16.

This Scripture reads, "And it shall come to pass, that every one that is left of all the nations which came against Jerusalem...." I think there will still be nations that come against Jerusalem, just as it has happened throughout Jerusalem's lifetime. The Christian Church is always ahead

of its time because the Christian Church walks with God
and not according to what man understands.

> *And it shall come to pass, that every one that is left of all
> the nations which came against Jerusalem shall even go
> up from year to year to worship the King, the Lord of
> hosts, and to keep the feast of tabernacles.*

> Zechariah 14:16

Most of us, as Christians, knew little about how to ob-
serve the Feast of Tabernacles in a scriptural manner
before 1980. Today, the government of Jewish Israel has
given the Christian community official status. Every year
the Feast of Tabernacles is kept by the Jews as a holy feast.
It has happened every year for more than 3,000 years.
Now, every year since 1980, when the International Christian Embassy, Jerusalem, began, thousands of Christians
from most of the nations worship together at one time
during the Feast of Tabernacles in Jerusalem and are accepted by the Jewish community.

As a part of this celebration, we are privileged to celebrate with the Jews, walking together down the main Jaffa
Street in the heart of Jerusalem, singing and comforting
God's people. I don't know of a higher glory and blessing
in obedience to God's Word than to march down the
main street of Jerusalem on Jaffa Street, and to express
our love to those people who are our heritage. They don't
realize that when we walk down their main street, their
Messiah walks down their main street too. We understand
though, and that's why it is easy for us to love them. Our
mission is to forgive them and to tell them that *their iniquity has been pardoned.*

Speak Comfortably to Jerusalem

Now we are also capable of fulfilling what Isaiah the prophet spoke about. Isaiah 40:1-2 says, "Comfort ye, comfort ye My people, saith your God. Speak ye comfortably to Jerusalem, and cry unto her, that her warfare is accomplished, that her iniquity is pardoned: for she hath received of the Lord's hand double for all her sins."

That sounds as though God has forgiven her. However, you could speak comfortably to Jerusalem only since 1980 when Jerusalem was *officially* declared the capital of Israel.

Is it possible to be forgiven and not know it? All Gentiles were in that condition when Jesus shed His blood 2,000 years ago. All the sins of all the people of the world are potentially forgiven. They're not all forgiven individually, for each one needs to confess or acknowledge them through repentance and confession of God's gift. But from God's perspective, all sins are forgiven and the price has been paid!

What if we could say, "All the Jews are forgiven"? As far as God is concerned, they have gone through sufficient punishment. They are all forgiven, except most don't know it.

In Bible days, King Nebuchadnezzar forced the Jews out of Israel, demolished their temple, destroyed their walls, and held them captive for 70 years. What made God come to the conclusion that 70 years was enough? We know that a remnant came back to their land and rebuilt their temple. They rebuilt the walls of Jerusalem and they remained there until the time of Jesus. It is obvious that God gave back their land and chose to forgive them. It is God who sovereignly forgives and determines the times.

In our own generation, we have seen God return the land to them once again. The fact that we know Jerusalem is under the control of Jewish Israel is evidence that we are living in the time when, from God's perspective, they have been forgiven. They have a rightful claim to their land and to their capital.

When the prophet Isaiah said, "Comfort ye, comfort ye My people," to whom was he referring? We know that Christians are God's people. He wouldn't be asking us to comfort ourselves. Isaiah is referring to the nation of Israel and he makes his reference explicit when he speaks about Jerusalem. The world is coming against Jerusalem and against Israel. He says, "Comfort ye, comfort ye My people." "My people" is the Jewish people who are still blinded. They are God's original ancient people. God intends for His people, we believers, who are capable of comforting, to go and " 'Comfort ye, comfort ye My people,' saith your God. 'Speak ye comfortably to Jerusalem.' "

I can comfort them only because I know that God has forgiven them. How do I know that God has forgiven them? They're back in their land. They have their capital. According to the Scriptures, *the time to comfort them is now.* Before 1980 I could not fulfill Isaiah 40:1. I couldn't have spoken comfort to Jerusalem if I knew three-fourths of the city was controlled by the Jordanian Arabs (Gentiles). When the Gentiles were in control, the Prophecy had not been fulfilled.

With the victory in 1967 (i.e., the Six-Day War), we see the fulfillment of what Jesus said. "Jerusalem shall be trodden down of the Gentiles, until the times of the Gentiles be fulfilled" (Luke 21:24b). So the time is here. It didn't happen in just one year, but we're in the fulfillment. It will be totally consummated when we see Jesus return from Heaven and set foot on the Mount of Olives. Then the time of the Gentiles will be totally consummated. Since receiving this understanding, I no longer have any fear of the Jews. I can stand by a rabbi or a Jew just as comfortably as I can stand by any of my Christian brothers or sisters.

What impresses them now is I talk in favor of their nation. You see, it is not only their nation, but it's yours and mine too. It is not only their capital city, but it also is my capital city. Israel is my fatherland. It's my heritage as a born-again believer. I know I have an obligation because I understand the time and the *signs of the time*. Since the time of the Gentiles is being fulfilled, God is putting the emphasis back on Israel as a people again.

It is important for the Church to understand this message because we are being affected by the ignorance and indifference that prevents the Church from carrying out its responsibility. That land contains the city from which God's Kingdom on earth will be ruled. The Kingdom of God will, ultimately, be ruled from Jerusalem.

If we really believe that Jesus Christ is coming back again, then we should take an interest in what is happening in Jerusalem. We should be involved in getting the land ready for her King.

Pray for the peace of Jerusalem.

Blessed are the peacemakers: for they shall be called the children of God. (Matt. 5:9)

Summary

Now that you have read this book, don't you agree with me that now is only the beginning of greater divine events in this time? The brightness of His light is penetrating the darkness and all ungodliness.

Perhaps you may be one of God's special, called-out, chosen ones to serve in His army to open the blindness and ungodliness that prevails upon the land that God calls "My land."

Can we justify ourselves and sit back in personal comfort, ignoring the clear unveiled vision for the Deliverer to come and exude grace—grace upon a people whose time has come to be set free? We know who the Deliverer is, as well as His location.

Shouldn't we do even as He did when the Father sent Him to the land of Israel 2,000 years ago and practice the same grace? Today we are a mighty army, invincible, prepared, our loins girded with truth, and anointed with the brightness of His glory!

When you meet the Arab, seed of Abraham, or the Jew, seed of Abraham, know that we are all in the same family. We too are of our father Abraham. So let the mercies of God flow richly and freely from your heart, forgiving and blessing those whose time has come.

> *But in the last days it shall come to pass, that the mountain of the house of the Lord shall be established in the top of the mountains, and it shall be exalted above the hills; and people shall flow unto it.*
>
> *And many nations shall come, and say, Come, and let us go up to the mountain of the Lord, and to the house of the God of Jacob; and He will teach us of His ways, and we will walk in His paths: for the law shall go forth of Zion, and the word of the Lord from Jerusalem.*

Micah 4:1-2

Books by Gerald Derstine

Following the Fire
(Softcover) $9.95
An autobiographical account of the trials and triumphs of Gerald
Derstine's ministry, from the phenomenal 1954 revival at White
Earth Indian Reservation to the beginning years of the Florida
Christian Retreat.

Present Time Miracles in Israel and West Bank
Territories $4.00
From 1980 to 1991, chronologically, you will see the miraculous
hand of God moving in the Bible lands. The signs and wonders
have accelerated since 1988—Israel's 40th anniversary. Bible days
are upon us.

The Kingdom of God Is at Hand $5.00
God's Kingdom has come and is coming. Read God's plan for the
Church now. Also available in Spanish.

Destined to Mature $5.00
A must for every Christian worker, pastor, Sunday school teacher
or layman seeking deeper truth. Your life will be enriched through
chapters such as "Finding Your Place" and "Discerning God's
Thoughts."

Visitation of God to the Mennonites $3.00
This book is a testimony of the beginning of Gerald and Beulah
Derstine's ministry, and the spiritual awakening among the Men-
nonite people of the United States and Canada.

God Speaks Today $3.00
A compilation of visions and prophecies given in recent years regarding the end-time plan of God.

To Receive the Holy Spirit $3.00
A study given by Reverend Derstine teaching the Christian the purpose of the Holy Spirit in the life of the believer and how to yield to receive. Included also is a discourse on the gift of tongues.

God, How Practical Can You Get? $5.00
A how-to handbook for Christians based on the Book of James. Eleven chapters, including "The Joy of Temptation" and "Faith That Works."

Women's Place in the Church $3.00
Read how Spirit-filled women are commissioned to obey the voice of God. Women fill a very important role in the ministry of the Church. The Scriptures are clear on the subject.

Lively Living $4.00
A commentary given on First Peter. Nine chapters, including "The Reward of Suffering"; "Husband and Wife Relationships" and "Happiness Through Misunderstanding."

One-hour video tapes VHS
Awakening In Israel: Part I
Awakening In Israel: Part II
$25 for one or $40 for two
Hear teachings by Gerald Derstine concerning prophetic fulfillments in the Holy Land. Also see and hear about present day signs and wonders taking place in Israel. A must for every Bible teacher and Christian worker.

Mail orders to:

**Israel Affairs International
1200 Glory Way Boulevard
Bradenton, FL 34202**

Please add $2 for postage and handling.

**PERCEIVING THE WHEEL
OF GOD**

by Dr. Mark Hanby.

Many have wondered about
the purpose of suffering. In
this book Dr. Hanby provides
us with an anointed answer to
that question. As unformed
clay yields to the squeezing
fingers of the potter, so must
we perceive and yield to the
wheel of God.

TPB-112p. ISBN 1-56043-109-1
Retail $7.95

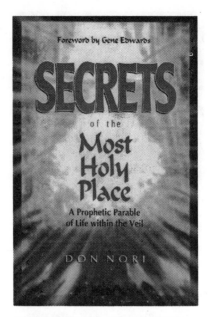

SECRETS OF THE MOST HOLY PLACE

by Don Nori.

Here is a prophetic parable you will read again and again. The winds of God are blowing, drawing you to His Life within the Veil of the Most Holy Place. There you begin to see as you experience a depth of relationship your heart has yearned for. This book is a living, dynamic experience with God!

TPB-182p. ISBN 1-56043-076-1
Retail $7.95